Convection Oven Cooking *for* All Seasons

From Appetizers to Desserts, Breads, Snacks and More—Convection Oven Cooking for Every Day of the Week

Convection Oven Cooking *for* All Seasons

From Appetizers to Desserts, Breads, Snacks and More—Convection Oven Cooking for Every Day of the Week

Debra Marie Thomas

Pascoe Publishing, Inc.
Rocklin, California

Cover design by Knockout Books
Page Design by Melanie Haage Design

Published in the United States of America by
Pascoe Publishing, Inc.
Rocklin, California
http://www.pascoepublishing.com

ISBN: 1-929862-19-9

03 04 05 06 10 9 8 7 6 5 4 3 2 1

Printed in the United States of America

Table of Contents

Chapter 3 Breakfast & Brunch Delicacies

Chapter 4 Hearty Meat, Poultry & Seafood Main Dishes

Chapter 6 Delightful Bakery Breads, Muffins & Rolls

Chapter 7 Luscious Convection Oven Desserts

For years experienced cooks have known that convection ovens are the optimal appliance for preparing delicious baked goods. Why? The method of circulating hot air throughout the oven ensures that foods are cooked evenly, producing a golden brown finish—resulting in a fabulous and delicious dish every time!

We are pleased to bring this exciting new book, *Convection Oven Cooking for All Seasons* to you and we hope that you will enjoy the recipes within these pages. You'll find one of our all-time favorite recipes, *Art's Favorite Rhubarb Brunch Cake*, included in the dessert chapter of this book—try it for family and friends!

Thank you for your interest in this series of books. We hope you'll let us know if you like these recipes!

If you are looking for some great Ultrex® pieces to add to your collection, please visit us at: www.hsn.com, keyword "Ultrex."

Sincerely,
Art & Maryann Krull

CHAPTER ONE

Introduction to Convection Oven Cooking

As the owner of a convection oven you have a remarkable appliance that produces fantastic foods. The convection oven cooks efficiently while producing baked goods with absolutely scrumptious flavors! This book is either the beginning of a cooking adventure for you, or it is part of the enjoyment that you are experiencing already as a convection oven cook. In the following pages you will find recipes for all types of foods—from appetizers and brunch breads to baked vegetables and luscious desserts. Frittatas bake to a delicate finish, vegetables caramelize to a beautiful brown translucence and meats are juicy and flavorful. *Herbed Tenderloin of Beef, Basil Asparagus with Portobello Mushrooms, Gingered Yeast Rolls* and *Chocolate Almond Macaroons* are some of the recipes that you will find in this cookbook. Seafood, meats, vegetables and breakfast foods will be baked to perfection in your convection oven.

A standard oven works on the basis of surrounding your baking food with hot air. This hot air flow is erratic and unevenly distributed. However, the convection oven has a fan in the back of the oven that circulates the hot air toward and around the food. The even distribution of the hot air through all parts of the oven shortens the amount of time needed for baking and produces excellent finished foods. This process allows for the convection oven to bake at a 25% lower oven temperature compared with the standard oven, as well as a 25% decrease in the amount of baking time. With the hot air circulating immediately and completely, the sugars in the vegetables begin to caramelize quickly, the meats roast to a hearty perfection and cookies bake to a uniform golden brown.

In a standard oven the food must be placed in the middle of the oven. This allows the hot air to circulate as best it can around the food. This is not an important factor for the convection oven. Actually, the convection oven is most efficient when baking more than one dish at a time. The hot air surrounds all of the baking dishes evenly and this saves energy. You can bake meats and vegetables or breads and egg dishes together when they have the same baking times and temperatures.

As you read through the use and care manual that came with your convection oven, you will see that this oven is very easy to use. It's truly a joy to operate, whether you are a new cook or an experienced chef! Be sure to watch your cooking times carefully. The convection oven cooks fast so the food will be done sooner rather than later. Remember to always use oven mitts when putting food into the oven or taking it out. Always be aware of any children who may be helping or who are nearby when the oven is in use. This appliance should not be used by children unless they are supervised by an adult.

Convection ovens are so versatile that you can select from a wide variety of bakeware pans for baking in the oven, including the new plastic-wrap ovenware. Baking pans with low sides are possibly the best option because they allow the food to receive as much heat as possible and the lower-sided pans work especially well when roasting meats. Specialty bakeware and cooking accessories are generally safe for the convection oven and can be used as they would be with a conventional oven. When using items such as parchment on a cookie sheet, the blowing air from the fan will cause the paper to puff up so the edges of the paper should be secured to the cookie sheet using metal spoons or weights. Also, because some fans are quite strong, delicate bakery foods such as meringues and cream toppings may be affected. Check your most delicate foods carefully during the cooking process to determine that the air is circulating under optimum conditions around such foods.

The recipes in this book are proportioned for the full size convection oven. If you have a countertop model, reduce the recipes as needed, use a baking dish that fits your oven and watch the baking times carefully. The actual baking time may be shorter than suggested in the recipe. When roasting meats, purchase the size of roast that will fit into your convection oven and then use the recommended meat-roasting times in your oven's manual, or check the roasting meat carefully as it cooks.

Let's start baking some exceptional foods!

CHAPTER TWO

Outstanding Starters & Snacks

Appetizers are wonderful foods for that special party, the "Monday Night Football" group or a quick get-together with friends. The convection oven bakes these appetizers to absolute perfection. There are choices such as *Herb & Mushroom Clam Shells, Italian Bruschetta, Smoked Ham Puffs* and *Nutty Blue Cheese Rolls*. Most of the appetizers in this chapter can be baked on baking sheets. This allows the hot air circulated by the convection oven fan to reach each individual appetizer. Each appetizer bakes to the same golden brown as the others, adding eye-appeal to their presentation on a serving tray.

The roll and puff recipes that are included in this chapter take a bit of time to prepare—and they are worth it. Your convection oven bakes the puff pastry to a crispy crust that flakes easily. Be sure to keep the unbaked pastry sheets covered until it is time to work with them. Their moisture makes them pliable. The butter that is brushed onto the pastry sheets evaporates quickly in the convection oven, making the crispy edges and flaky crusts. Try *Chicken & Spinach Phyllo Rolls* and *Puff Pastry Cheese Straws*.

For those quick snacks that kids love, it's got to be *Pepperoni Pizza Sticks, Home-Baked Tortilla Chips,* and *Potato Skins and More!* Quick, easy and filling, these snacks bring satisfaction to any hungry, active family. And, they are perfect for a group of friends, too! With these recipes, you can have snacks and appetizers available fresh out of your convection oven. A treat for all!

Italian Bruschetta

6 slices fresh French bread, cut in 1/2-inch slices

6 T. extra virgin olive oil

2 cloves garlic, minced

1 Roma tomato, peeled, seeded and cubed

1 sprig fresh basil, finely chopped

1 t. dried oregano

1 sprig fresh thyme, finely chopped

1/4 t. salt

1/4 t. black pepper

2 T. Parmesan cheese, shredded

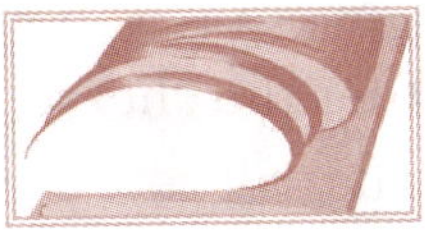

Preheat the convection oven to 375°F. Place the bread slices on the oven tray and toast them in the convection oven until they are lightly browned. Remove the pan from the convection oven and spread the olive oil and the garlic evenly over each piece of toast. Layer the Roma tomato cubes on the toast. Sprinkle the basil, oregano and the thyme on the top of the tomato. Season with the salt and pepper as desired. Drizzle olive oil over each bruschetta. Sprinkle with the Parmesan cheese. Place the pan back into the convection oven to warm the cheese until it melts and the edges of the bread begin to brown. Serve immediately. Makes 6 slices.

Caraway Bread Sticks

- 1 egg, beaten
- 1 T. water
- 1 t. Dijon mustard
- 3/4 c. Swiss cheese, finely shredded
- 1/4 c. sweet onion, finely chopped
- 2 t. fresh parsley, snipped
- 1 1/2 t. caraway seed
- 1/4 t. garlic salt
- 1 sheet 17 1/4 oz. package frozen puff pastry, thawed

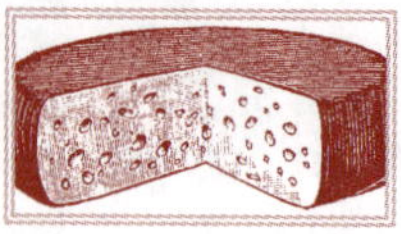

In a small bowl, combine the egg, water and the mustard. Set aside. In a medium bowl, stir together the cheese, onion, parsley, caraway seed and the garlic salt.

Preheat the convection oven to 325°F. On a lightly floured board, unfold the pastry sheet. Generously brush the pastry with the egg mixture. Sprinkle the cheese mixture lengthwise over half of the pastry rectangle. Fold the other half of the pastry sheet over the top of the cheese mixture, matching edges and corners. Press the edges to seal. Brush the top of the pastry with the egg mixture. With a sharp knife, cut the pastry crosswise into ½-inch wide strips. Twist each strip several times and place them 1 inch apart on a greased baking sheet, pressing the ends down onto the sheet. Bake in the convection oven for 18 to 20 minutes, or until lightly browned. Serve warm. Makes 18 bread sticks.

Cheese & Green Chile Bake

- 4 eggs
- 1/2 t. baking powder
- 1/4 c. all-purpose flour (whole wheat flour can be substituted)
- 1/2 t. dry mustard
- 1 c. cottage cheese
- 1 c. cheddar cheese, shredded
- 1 c. Jack cheese, shredded
- 1/4 c. butter, melted
- 8 oz. can green chilies, chopped
- 1 avocado, sliced
- 1/4 c. prepared salsa

Preheat the convection oven to 325°F. In a mixing bowl beat the eggs. Add the baking powder, flour and the dry mustard. Stir in the cheeses, melted butter and the green chilies. The batter will be slightly lumpy. Lightly coat a 9-inch square baking pan with cooking spray. Pour the batter into the baking pan and bake in the convection oven for 25 to 30 minutes. Serve warm. Garnish with the sliced avocado and the salsa. Serves 9.

Herb & Mushroom Clam Shells

7 1/2-oz. can minced clams
4 T. vegetable oil
2 T. scallions, including the tender greens, minced
3 T. fresh parsley, minced
1 t. capers, drained and chopped
1/4 c. mushrooms, finely chopped
2 T. lemon juice (fresh is best)
4 T. saltine crackers, crushed
1/2 hard boiled egg, mashed
1/4 t. salt
1/4 t. ground black pepper
4 scallop shells, cleaned and dried

Preheat the convection oven to 400°F. Drain the clams and set aside on a paper towel. In a large sauté pan, heat the oil and add the scallions, parsley, capers and the mushrooms. Sauté over medium heat for about 5 minutes. Remove from the heat and stir in the lemon juice and the cracker crumbs. Add the mashed boiled egg and the clams. Stir gently. Season with salt and pepper.

Lightly grease 4 scallop shells. Fill the shells with equal portions of the clam mixture. Bake in the preheated convection oven for 4 to 5 minutes. Serve immediately. Serves 4.

Cheese Crinkle Crackers

- 2 c. sharp cheddar cheese, shredded
- 1/2 c. butter
- 1 1/2 c. all-purpose flour
- 1/4 t. salt
- 1/4 t. ground red pepper

In a large mixing bowl, combine the shredded cheese and the butter. Let this stand for 1 hour to come to room temperature. Beat the cheese mixture with an electric mixer and combine well. Stir in the flour, salt and the red pepper. Divide the dough into 2 halves. Shape the halves into two 7-inch logs. Wrap each log in plastic wrap and chill for at least one hour. Preheat the convection oven to 325°F. With a knife or a crinkle cutter, slice the cheese logs into ¼-inch slices. Place the slices on an ungreased baking sheet. Bake in the convection oven for 15 minutes. Remove the crackers to a cooling rack. When completely cooled, store in an airtight container. Makes 4½ dozen crackers.

Chicken & Spinach Phyllo Rolls

5 oz. can cooked chicken, drained and flaked

1 c. cheddar cheese, shredded

10 oz. package frozen chopped spinach, thawed

4 oz. cream cheese with chives and onion

1/2 c. walnuts, chopped

1 T. dry sherry (or water)

1/2 t. Worcestershire sauce

1/4 t. ground nutmeg

8 sheets frozen phyllo dough, thawed

1/3 c. butter, melted

In a large mixing bowl combine the chicken, cheddar cheese, spinach, cream cheese, walnuts, sherry, Worcestershire sauce and the nutmeg. Preheat the convection oven to 375°F. Place one sheet of the phyllo on a lightly floured board. Gently brush the phyllo with some melted butter. Place another phyllo sheet on top of the buttered sheet. Brush the top phyllo with butter. As you work, cover the unused phyllo with a damp cloth to prevent it from drying. Spoon about ½ cup of the filling evenly down the long side of the phyllo, leaving a 2-inch space between the edge of the phyllo and the filling. Leave a 1 inch boundary on both sides of the phyllo. Fold the 2 inch phyllo edge over the filling and fold in the 1 inch sides. Loosely roll like a jelly-roll from the long side of the phyllo. Place the phyllo roll, seam side down, on an ungreased baking sheet. Repeat with the remaining phyllo and filling. Brush the tops of the phyllo rolls with butter. Use a sharp knife and score the rolls at 1½ inch intervals. Bake in the convection oven for 15 minutes or until they are golden brown. Let the rolls stand for 5 minutes and then slice. Serve warm. Makes 36 pieces.

The phyllo rolls can be made 6 to 8 hours ahead of time and chilled until ready to heat and serve.

Chinese Pork & Vegetable Pockets

- 1 lb. ground pork sausage
- 1 T. garlic, minced
- 11/2 T. Chinese hot mustard
- 2 T. rice wine vinegar
- 1 T. soy sauce
- 1 T. sesame oil
- 1 T. Chinese hot oil
- 8 oz. can water chestnuts, drained and finely chopped
- 2 T. fresh parsley, finely chopped
- 1 T. green onions, finely chopped
- 1 tube sourdough refrigerator biscuits (10 biscuits)

- 1 egg yolk
- 2 t. cream
- 1 T. sesame seeds

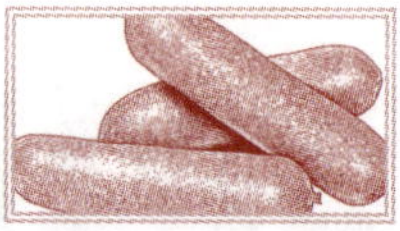

Sauté in a medium skillet, the ground pork sausage, garlic, Chinese hot mustard, rice vinegar, soy sauce and the oils. When the sausage is browned add the water chestnuts, parsley and green onions. Mix well. Cool to room temperature. Preheat the convection oven to 350°F. Coat a baking sheet with cooking spray. On a lightly floured surface, roll out the each of the biscuits to ¼-inch thickness. Cut into 2½-inch rounds. Roll each biscuit round to a thickness of ⅛-inch. Place 1 tablespoon of the sausage mixture into the center of the biscuit. Gather up the ends of the dough and pinch it to form a sealed ball. Place these on the baking sheet. Mix the egg yolk and the cream together into an egg wash. Brush this wash on the top of each roll and sprinkle with sesame seeds. Bake for 12 to 15 minutes until the rolls are nicely golden brown. Serve warm. Makes 10 rolls.

Baltimore Crab Canapés

7 oz. can crab meat, drained
1/4 c. celery, minced
2 t. prepared mustard
4 t. sweet pickle relish
2 green onions, finely chopped
1/2 c. mayonnaise
16 crackers of your choice

Preheat the convection oven to 350°F. Rinse the crab meat under cold water and remove any cartilage. Place the crab meat in a medium bowl and flake with a fork. Add the celery, mustard, pickle relish, green onions and the mayonnaise to the crab meat. Mix well. Spread about 1 tablespoon of the crab mixture on each cracker. Place the crackers on an ungreased baking sheet. Bake for 30 to 45 seconds, or until the crab appetizers are cooked through and hot. Serve immediately. Makes 16 canapés.

Crab & Onion Stuffed Mushrooms

- 1 T. butter or margarine
- 1 clove garlic, minced
- 4 green onions, chopped
- 6 oz. can crab meat, drained and flaked
- 1 c. dry bread crumbs
- 5 oz. can water chestnuts, drained and chopped
- 1/2 c. mayonnaise
- 2 T. fresh parsley, chopped
- 1/4 t. salt
- 1/4 t. black pepper
- 12 medium size mushrooms

Preheat the convection oven to 325°F. In a frying pan melt the butter and sauté the minced garlic and the green onions. Add the flaked crab meat and the bread crumbs. Remove from the heat. Add the water chestnuts, mayonnaise, parsley and the salt and pepper. Gently mix with a spoon until the mixture sticks together.

Quickly wash the mushrooms and pat dry. Remove the stems. Fill each mushroom with the crab mixture creating the shape of a ball. Place filled mushrooms on an ungreased baking sheet. Bake for 25 minutes. The mushroom caps should begin to brown. Makes 12 stuffed mushrooms.

Cracked Pepper Crackers

1 T. black peppercorns, crushed
1 T. salt
1/4 c. vegetable oil
2 T. horseradish
1 t. red pepper sauce
2 c. canned tomato juice
7 c. bread flour

Mix the peppercorns and salt in a large bowl. Add the vegetable oil, horseradish, red pepper sauce and the tomato juice. Mix thoroughly. Add in the flour, 1 cup at a time, until the dough is formed. Wrap the dough in plastic wrap and chill for at least 1 hour. Preheat the convection oven to 325°F. On a lightly floured surface roll the dough as thin as possible. Cut into 2-inch squares and place on a parchment lined baking pan. Bake for 8 to 10 minutes until the crackers are crisp. Place on a cooling rack and then store in an airtight container. Makes 3 to 4 dozen.

Nutty Blue Cheese Rolls

- 2/3 c. walnuts, finely chopped
- 1/3 c. blue cheese, crumbled
- 1 T. fresh parsley, finely snipped
- 1/4 t. black pepper
- 1 refrigerated ready-to-use piecrust
- 1 T. milk
- 2 t. Parmesan cheese, grated

Preheat the convection oven to 375°F. In a mixing bowl, combine the walnuts, blue cheese, parsley and the black pepper. On a lightly floured board, unfold the piecrust according to the package directions. Spread the cheese mixture evenly over the crust. Cut the pastry circle into 12 wedges. Starting at the wide ends, loosely roll up the wedges. Place the rolls tip side down on a greased baking pan. Brush the rolls lightly with milk. Sprinkle the rolls with Parmesan cheese and additional parsley. Bake in the convection oven for 15 minutes until golden brown. Cool slightly on a wire rack and serve warm. The rolls can be covered and refrigerated for up to 24 hours before baking, if desired. Makes 12 rolls.

Pepperoni Pizza Sticks

- 11 oz. can soft bread sticks
- 24 pepperoni pieces, thinly sliced
- 2 T. Parmesan cheese, grated
- 1/2 t. dried Italian seasoning
- 1/4 t. garlic powder
- 1/2 c. prepared pizza sauce, heated

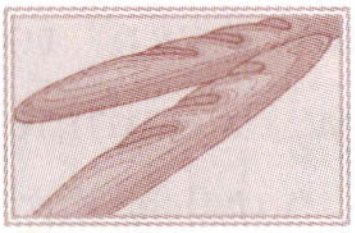

Preheat the convection oven to 325°F. Unroll the bread sticks on a lightly floured surface. Place 3 pepperoni slices in a single layer over ½ of each bread stick. Fold the remaining half of the bread stick over the top of the pepperoni. Seal the end of the bread stick and twist. Place the bread sticks on an ungreased baking sheet. Combine the Parmesan cheese, Italian seasoning and the garlic powder. Sprinkle this mixture evenly over each bread stick. Bake for 15 to 20 minutes, until golden brown. Serve the pizza sticks accompanied by the heated pizza sauce. Makes 8 pizza sticks.

Potato Skins and More

6 large russet potatoes
2 t. vegetable oil
1 t. chili powder
2 dashes red pepper sauce (optional)
2/3 c. Canadian style bacon, chopped
1 tomato, finely chopped
1 t. jalapeño peppers, chopped
2 T. green onions, finely chopped
1 c. cheddar cheese, shredded
1/2 c. sour cream

Bake the potatoes in the convection oven at 400°F for 60 minutes or until tender. Cool. Halve each potato lengthwise. Scoop out the inside of each potato half, leaving a ¼-inch thick shell. Save the inside of the potatoes for other uses. Combine the vegetable oil, chili powder and the red pepper sauce. Brush the insides of the potato skins with this mixture. Cut the potato halves in half again lengthwise. Place these potato quarters on a greased baking sheet. Top the potatoes with the bacon, tomato, jalapeños and the green onion. Layer the cheese on top. If desired, cover and chill these potato quarters for up to 24 hours. Bake in the convection oven at 400°F for 10 to 12 minutes or until the cheese is melted and the filling is hot. Serve with sour cream. Makes 24 wedges.

Puff Pastry Cheese Straws

17 1/4-oz. pkg. frozen puff pastry, thawed

1 egg white, lightly beaten

paprika to taste

cayenne pepper (optional)

1 c. Parmesan cheese, finely shredded

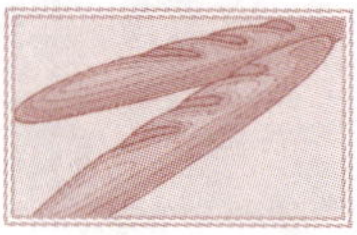

Preheat the convection oven to 350°F. Open one sheet of the puff pastry onto a cutting board. Lightly brush the surface of the pastry with the egg white. Sprinkle onto the pastry the paprika and the cayenne pepper. Evenly coat the surface of the pastry with ½ cup of the Parmesan cheese. Roll a floured rolling pin over the cheese to gently press the cheese into the puff pastry. Cut the pastry lengthwise into strips ½-inch in width. Gently twist each strip several times. Cover a baking sheet with parchment paper and place the strips on the paper. Repeat with the remaining sheet of puff pastry. Bake in the convection oven for 12 to 14 minutes, or until the pastry is golden in color. Cool on a wire rack. Serve the same day, or store in an airtight container. Makes 36 Cheese Straws.

Home-Baked Tortilla Chips

8 whole corn tortillas
1 T. corn oil
3 T. lime juice, bottled or fresh
1 t. cumin powder
1 t. chili powder
1 t. salt

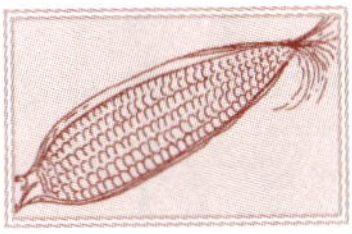

Preheat the convection oven to 325°F. Cut the tortillas into 8 chip-size wedges. Arrange the tortillas on a baking sheet in a single layer. Using a mister, spray the tortillas with the corn oil and the lime juice. Combine the cumin powder, chili powder and the salt in a small bowl. Sprinkle the chips with this seasoning. Bake in the convection oven for 15 minutes, or until they are crispy. Rotate the pan half-way through the baking time. Makes 64 chips.

Garlic Chicken Pizza

- 12 oz. chicken breast halves, skinless and boneless
- 1/2 c. green onion, sliced
- 2 cloves garlic, minced
- 2 T. rice wine vinegar (you may substitute white wine vinegar)
- 2 T. soy sauce
- 2 T. olive oil
- 1/2 t. crushed red pepper
- 1/4 t. black pepper
- 1 T. cornstarch
- 1 12-inch Italian bread shell
- 1/2 c. Jack cheese, shredded
- 1/2 c. mozzarella cheese, shredded
- 2 T. pine nuts or sliced almonds

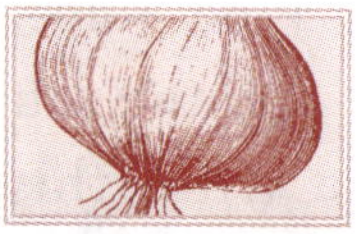

Rinse and dry the chicken. Slice the chicken into ½-inch pieces. In a small bowl, combine half of the green onions, the garlic, rice vinegar, soy sauce, 1 tablespoon olive oil, red pepper and the black pepper. Add the chicken pieces and stir to coat the chicken with the marinade. Let this mixture stand for 30 minutes at room temperature. Drain and reserve the marinade. Preheat the convection oven to 375°F. In a large skillet, heat the remaining olive oil and stir-fry the chicken pieces for about 3 minutes. Stir the cornstarch into the reserved marinade and add to the skillet. Cook and stir the chicken mixture until it is bubbly. Remove from the heat.

Spread the chicken mixture evenly over the top of the bread shell. Sprinkle the chicken with the Jack cheese and the mozzarella cheese. Bake in the convection oven for 12 minutes. Top the pizza with the remaining green onions and the nuts. Continue baking for 2 minutes. Remove the pizza from the convection oven to a cutting board and slice into wedges. Serves 4-6.

Honey & Garlic Spareribs

- 3 lbs. pork spareribs
- 1/4 t. garlic salt
- 1/2 c. honey
- 3 T. cider vinegar
- 1/4 t. black pepper
- 1/4 c. soy sauce
- 3 cloves garlic, minced

Preheat the convection oven to 325°F. Season the spareribs with the garlic salt. Cut the spareribs into individual ribs and arrange in a 9" x 13" baking dish. Cover with foil and bake in the convection oven for 1 hour. Drain off the liquid. In a saucepan, combine the honey, cider vinegar, black pepper, soy sauce and the garlic and simmer for 5 minutes. Pour this honey mixture over the ribs and bake uncovered for 30 minutes. Baste every 10 minutes. Makes 20 appetizers.

Smoked Ham Puffs

- 17 1/4-oz. package puff pastry, thawed
- 4 T. apricot jam
- 2 c. smoked ham, finely chopped
- 1 c. pepper Jack cheese, shredded
- 2 eggs, lightly beaten

Preheat the convection oven to 375°F. Coat a baking sheet with non-stick spray. On a lightly floured surface, lay out one sheet of pastry dough. Cut the dough into 12 even squares. Brush each square with apricot jam. In the center of each square layer the ham and the cheese. Fold over the dough on each square and press the edges to seal. Brush lightly with the beaten eggs. Repeat the process with the second sheet of puff pastry. Place the puffs on the baking sheet and bake for 15 minutes until they are brown and puffy. Serve warm. Makes 24 appetizers

CHAPTER THREE

Breakfast & Brunch Delicacies

Ah! Morning time...and the day waits with so much to do. Now is the time to get energized with some delicious breakfast foods. This chapter has many types of recipes for the morning meal that are especially tasty when baked in the convection oven. Some of these foods are prepared the night before and refrigerated until the morning when they bake to a fresh and hot goodness. There are recipes for breads, muffins and coffee cakes that provide a light meal with juice, fruit and coffee. And, there are the breakfast recipes that will bring everyone to the table in a hurry—*Italian Potatoes & Eggs, Crab & Swiss Cheese Quiche* and *Ham & Eggs Breakfast Burritos*.

If you are having guests for brunch, try *Apples & Spice Baked Toast, Tropical Puff Pancake* or *Maple Syrup Baked Pears*. Add to these specialties a delicious *Cinnamon Nut Coffee Cake* or *Rich Blueberry Streusel Coffee Cake*. And, the *Chocolate Glazed Almond Biscotti* is the perfect companion for a hot cup of coffee.

These recipes are all easy to prepare and bake and each adds a certain touch of "specialness" to your morning. And, your convection oven will bake all of these recipes to their best, helping you provide your best. So, "Welcome to Morning!"

Apples & Spice Baked Toast

- 1 large loaf French or Italian bread
- 8 large eggs
- 1 c. sugar
- 3 1/2 c. milk
- 1 T. vanilla extract
- 6 to 8 tart apples
- 3 t. ground cinnamon
- 1 t. ground nutmeg
- 2 T. butter

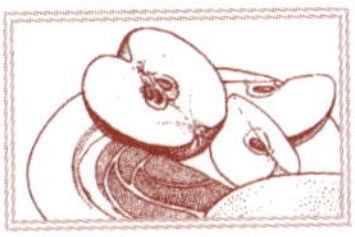

Slice the bread into 1½-inch slices. Spray a 9" x 13" pan with cooking spray. Place the bread into the pan, arranging the bread so that it fits tightly. In a mixing bowl, beat together the eggs, ½ cup sugar, milk and the vanilla. Pour half of this egg mixture over the bread. Peel, core and slice the apples. Place the sliced apples on top of the bread to cover. Pour the remaining egg mixture over the apples. In a small bowl, mix the remaining ½ cup sugar, cinnamon, and the nutmeg. Sprinkle this over the top of the apples. Dot the apples with butter. Cover and refrigerate overnight.

In the morning, uncover the dish and bake in the convection oven at 325°F for 1 hour. The toast will rise and brown nicely. Remove the toast from the oven and allow it to rest for 5 to 10 minutes before cutting. Serve with warm maple syrup, whipped cream and/or fruit. Serves 8.

Blueberry Coffee Cake

Cake:
2 c. all purpose flour
3/4 c. sugar
2 1/2 t. baking powder
3/4 t. salt
1/4 c. shortening
3/4 c. milk
1 egg
2 c. blueberries, fresh or frozen

Crumb Topping:
1/4 c. sugar
2 T. all purpose flour
1/2 t. ground cinnamon
1/4 c. butter, softened

Glaze:
1/2 c. powdered sugar
1/4 t. vanilla extract
1 1/2 t. hot water

Preheat the convection oven to 350°F. Grease a 9 to 10-inch springform pan. In a mixing bowl combine the flour, sugar, baking powder, salt, shortening, milk and the egg. Beat for 30 seconds. Carefully stir in the blueberries. Spread the batter in the pan evenly.

In a small bowl combine the sugar, flour, cinnamon and the soft butter until it is crumbly. Sprinkle this over the top of the batter. Bake this cake in the convection oven for 45 to 50 minutes or until a toothpick inserted in the center of the cake comes out clean. Remove the cake from the springform pan and cool for 10 to 15 minutes. Drizzle with the glaze. Serve warm.

In a small bowl blend the powdered sugar, vanilla and the hot water. Drizzle over the cake. Serves 8 to 10.

Rich Blueberry Streusel Coffee Cake

2 1/2 c. all purpose flour
3/4 c. sugar
1 t. packed brown sugar
1/2 t. salt
3/4 c. vegetable oil
1 1/4 c. buttermilk
1 large egg
1 t. baking soda
1 t. water
1 c. blueberries, fresh or frozen
1/2 c. pecans, chopped
2 t. ground cinnamon

Preheat the convection oven to 300°F. Grease a 9" x 9" pan. In a large bowl, mix together the flour, sugar, brown sugar, salt and the oil. Set aside ½ cup of this mixture for the streusel. Add the buttermilk and the egg to the flour mixture in the large bowl. Stir until the ingredients are moistened. In a small bowl combine the baking soda and the water and add it to the buttermilk batter. Gently fold the blueberries into the batter and spread the batter into the pan.

Stir together the reserved ½ cup streusel mix, pecans and the cinnamon. Sprinkle this over the top of the batter. Bake in the convection oven for 45 minutes, or until a wooden pick inserted in the middle of the cake comes out clean. Serves 6.

Breakfast Supreme

- 1/4 c. butter or margarine, melted
- 24 oz. bag of frozen hash brown potatoes
- 1 small sweet onion, chopped
- 1 small green pepper, chopped
- 2–3 medium tomatoes, chopped
- 1/4 t. salt
- 1/4 t. black pepper
- 3/4 lb. smoked ham, cubed
- 12 eggs, beaten
- 3 c. cheddar cheese, shredded

Pour the melted butter into a 9" x 13" baking pan. Spread the frozen hash browns on the bottom of the pan. Sprinkle the chopped vegetables over the hash browns and salt and pepper to taste. Sprinkle the ham over the potatoes and the vegetables. This can be covered and refrigerated overnight.

Preheat the convection oven to 325°F. Pour the beaten eggs over the top of the potatoes and ham. Bake in the convection oven for 45 minutes. Remove the pan from the oven and sprinkle the cheese evenly over the top of the baked potato and egg. Return the pan to the convection oven and bake for another 5 to 10 minutes until the cheese is hot and bubbly. Remove the breakfast casserole from the oven and allow it to cool for 5 minutes. Serves 8.

Cherry Almond Coffee Cake

- 2 c. all purpose flour
- 1 t. baking powder
- 1 t. baking soda
- 1/2 t. salt
- 1/2 c. unsalted butter, at room temperature
- 1 c. sugar
- 2 large eggs
- 1 t. vanilla extract
- 1/2 t. almond extract
- 1 c. sour cream
- 1 c. canned cherry pie filling
- 1/2 c. almonds, unblanched and sliced

Grease an 8-inch springform pan. In a medium bowl, stir together the flour, baking powder, baking soda and the salt. In a large bowl, with an electric mixer, beat the butter until it is creamy. Add the sugar to the butter, ¼ cup at a time, beating well after each addition. When the butter mixture is light and fluffy, add the eggs, one at a time. Add the vanilla and almond extracts and mix well.

With the mixer on low, add the flour mixture in ½ cup portions, alternating with the sour cream in ⅓ cup portions. Beat just until the batter is smooth. Spoon half of the batter into the springform pan. Add half of the cherry pie filling to the batter and swirl it through the batter using a spatula. Spoon the remaining batter into the springform pan. Layer the remaining cherry pie filling on the top of the batter, but do not swirl. Sprinkle the batter with the almonds, pressing them into the surface lightly.

Bake in the convection oven at 325°F for 1 hour. The cake will be brown on top and shrink slightly from the sides of the pan. The cake is done when a wooden pick inserted in the center of the cake comes out clean. Let the cake cool for 15 minutes and then remove the pan sides. Serve warm. Serves 12.

South of the Border Breakfast

3 English muffins, split
2 T. butter
1 lb. ground sausage
4 1/2-oz. can chopped green chilies, drained
3 c. cheddar cheese, shredded
12 large eggs, lightly beaten
1 1/2 c. sour cream

Spread the English muffin halves with the butter. Place the muffin halves in a greased 9" x 13" baking pan, butter side down. Brown the sausage in a skillet. Drain. Layer half of the sausage over the English muffin halves. Cover the sausage with half of the chilies and then top the chilies with half of the cheese. Repeat the layers of the sausage, chilies and the cheese. Pour the lightly beaten eggs over the top of the layers. Cover the casserole and chill overnight or for 8 hours.

Remove the casserole from the refrigerator and let it stand for 30 minutes. Preheat the convection oven to 325°F. Bake the casserole uncovered for 35 to 40 minutes. Remove from the oven and cool for 5 minutes. Garnish with sour cream. Serves 8.

Cinnamon Nut Coffee Cake

Cake:

1/2 c. butter or margarine

1/2 c. sugar

1 egg, slightly beaten

1 c. all purpose flour

2 t. baking powder

1/2 t. salt

1 c. milk

1 t. vanilla extract

Topping:

1 c. brown sugar, packed

3 T. all purpose flour

2 t. ground cinnamon

4 T. butter or margarine

1/2 c. walnuts or pecans, finely chopped

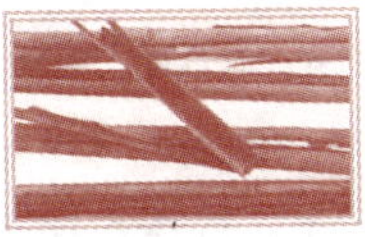

Spray a 9" x 9" baking pan with cooking spray. Preheat the convection oven to 325°F. In a medium bowl, combine the butter and the sugar. Beat in the egg. Sift together the flour, baking powder and the salt. Add this flour mixture to the creamed mixture alternately with the milk. Stir in the vanilla. Pour this batter into the baking pan.

In a small bowl, mix together the sugar, flour and the cinnamon. Cut in the butter with a fork or pastry blender. Spoon half of the topping over the batter and swirl with a spatula. Spoon the remaining topping over the batter and sprinkle with the nuts. Bake for 30 minutes. Cool slightly and serve. Serves 6.

Easy Eggs Rancheros

8 oz. can tomato sauce
1 t. chili powder
1/4 t. ground cumin
8 eggs
1/4 t. black pepper
1/4 t. paprika
1 c. cheddar cheese, shredded
4 prepared tostada shells

Preheat the convection oven to 325°F. In a lightly greased 9-inch pie pan, combine the tomato sauce, chili powder and the cumin. Break the eggs evenly over the sauce in the dish. Sprinkle the eggs with the pepper and the paprika.

Cover the pie pan with aluminum foil and bake for 15 to 20 minutes. Remove the aluminum foil, sprinkle the cheddar cheese over the eggs and bake an additional 5 minutes. To serve, spoon 2 eggs into a tostada shell or tortilla, and garnish as you wish. Serves 4.

Personal Breakfast Quiche

20 oz. package frozen shredded hash browns
1/3 c. butter or margarine, melted
4 c. cheddar cheese, shredded
6 c. milk
12 eggs
cayenne pepper to taste
garlic salt to taste

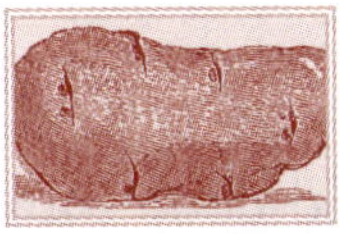

Preheat the convection oven to 325°F. Grease 12 jumbo muffin cups (5 to 6-inch diameter). Press the hash browns into the muffin cups to form a crust. Brush or drizzle the hash browns with the melted butter. Bake in the convection oven for 25 to 30 minutes.

Remove the muffin pans from the heat and evenly distribute the cheese in each of the muffin cups. Whisk together the milk, eggs, cayenne pepper and the garlic salt. Pour this egg mixture evenly over the cheese. Return the muffin pans back to the convection oven and continue baking for another 30 to 40 minutes. The quiche are done when a wooden pick inserted in the middle of each comes out clean. Cool slightly before removing the individual quiche from the pan. Serves 12.

Italian Potatoes & Eggs

6 large potatoes, boiled
2 T. vegetable oil
1/2 c. onion, chopped
1/2 t. basil
1/4 t. salt
1/4 t. black pepper
1 T. dried Italian seasoning
1 lb. bacon or sausage, cooked and crumbled
1 c. mozzarella cheese, shredded
10 eggs
1/2 c. water
1/2 c. cheddar cheese, shredded

Skin the boiled potatoes and chop into large square pieces. Heat the oil in a skillet and fry the potatoes with the onion, basil, salt, black pepper and the Italian seasoning. Fry until the potatoes brown lightly.

Preheat the convection oven to 375°F. Spray a 9" x 13" baking pan with non-stick spray. Layer the potatoes on the bottom of the pan. Crumble the bacon or sausage over the potatoes. Sprinkle the potatoes with the mozzarella cheese.

In a medium bowl, whisk together the eggs and the water. Pour this egg mixture over the potatoes. Bake for 40 minutes. This dish will puff up nicely. Remove the pan from the convection oven and sprinkle the dish with the cheddar cheese. Serve immediately. Serves 8.

Sour Cream Coffee Cake

Cake:

1/2 c. butter or margarine, softened

1 c. sugar

1/2 c. light brown sugar, packed

3 large eggs

1 c. sour cream

2 t. vanilla extract

2 1/2 c. all purpose flour

1 1/2 t. baking powder

1 1/2 t. baking soda

1/2 t. salt

Topping:

1 c. brown sugar, packed

2 t. ground cinnamon

1 t. ground nutmeg

1 c. pecans, chopped

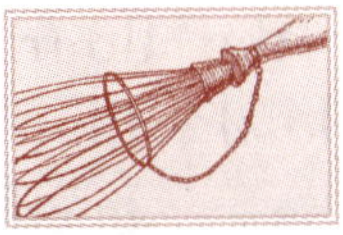

Preheat the convection oven to 325°F. In a large mixing bowl, cream the butter and the sugars. Add the eggs, sour cream and the vanilla extract. Mix well. In a medium bowl, combine the flour, baking powder, baking soda and the salt. Add the flour mixture to the creamed mixture and combine well.

In a small bowl, combine thoroughly all of the topping ingredients. Spray a 9" x 13" baking pan with cooking spray. Pour half of the cake batter into the pan. Sprinkle ½ of the topping mix over the batter. Layer the remaining batter and topping. Bake in the convection oven for 40 minutes. Cool and serve. Serves 12.

French Breakfast Muffins

Muffins:
1/2 c. sugar
1/3 c. butter or margarine
1 egg
1 1/2 c. all-purpose flour
1 1/2 t. baking powder
1/2 t. salt
3/4 t. ground nutmeg
1/2 c. milk

Topping:
1/2 c. sugar
1/4 t. ground cinnamon
6 T. butter, melted

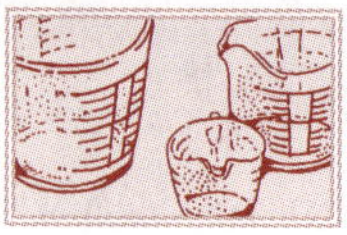

Preheat the convection oven to 350°F. Cream the sugar, butter and the egg completely. Sift together the flour, baking powder, salt and the nutmeg. Add the flour mixture alternately with the milk into the creamed sugar. Prepare 12 muffin cups by lightly coating with cooking spray or using paper muffin cup liners. Fill the muffin cups ⅔ full with the batter. Bake for 20 minutes. Insert a toothpick into the muffins to check for doneness.

Combine the topping ingredients and sprinkle over the warm muffins. Serves 12.

Crab & Swiss Cheese Quiche

3 eggs, slightly beaten
1 c. sour cream
1/2 t. Worcestershire sauce
3/4 t. salt
1 c. Swiss cheese, shredded
7 1/2-oz. can crab, drained and flaked
3 oz. can French-fried onions
2 9-inch baked pastry shells

Preheat the convection oven to 300°F. Combine the eggs, sour cream, Worcestershire sauce and the salt. Stir in the cheese, crab meat and the fried onions. Pour this mixture evenly into the 2 baked pastry shells. Bake for 1 hour or until the quiche are set. Cut each quiche into 8 pieces and serve while warm. Serves 16.

Chocolate Glazed Almond Biscotti

1 c. blanched whole almonds

3 eggs

1 t. vanilla extract

1/2 t. almond extract

1 T. lemon or orange zest, if desired

2 c. all-purpose flour

3/4 c. sugar

1 t. baking powder

1/8 t. salt

Glaze:

3 oz. semi-sweet or white chocolate

1 t. vegetable shortening

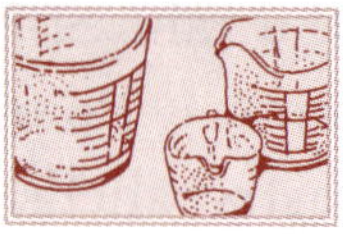

Preheat the convection oven to 350°F. Place the almonds on a baking sheet and toast the almonds for 6 to 8 minutes, or until lightly browned. Cool and chop coarsely.

Lightly grease a baking sheet. In a small bowl, beat together the eggs, vanilla extract and the almond extract. Add the lemon or orange zest, if desired. Set aside.

In a large bowl, combine the flour, sugar, baking soda and the salt. Gradually add the egg mixture and beat until the dough forms. Add the almonds. With floured hands, divide the dough in half and roll each half into a log, 10 inches long and 2 inches wide. Transfer the logs to the baking sheet.

Reduce the temperature of the oven to 300°F and bake for 30 to 35 minutes until the logs are firm to the touch. Remove from the oven and cool on a wire rack for about 10 minutes. Transfer the logs to a cutting board. With a serrated knife, cut the logs diagonally into slices 1½-inch wide and arrange the slices on the baking sheet, cut side down. Bake 10 to 12 minutes. Turn the slices over and bake another 10 minutes. Remove from the oven and cool. Prepare the glaze as follows:

Melt the chocolate and the vegetable shortening together in double boiler. Heat slowly to a simmer until smooth, stirring constantly. Spread the glaze on one side of each biscotti piece. Makes 30 biscotti. Store in an airtight container.

Tropical Puff Pancake

4 large eggs
1 c. milk
1 c. all-purpose flour
6 T. butter or margarine
1 firm ripe mango
1 firm ripe papaya
3 T. orange marmalade
1 T. lemon juice
1 1/2 c. raspberries, rinsed and drained
flaked coconut

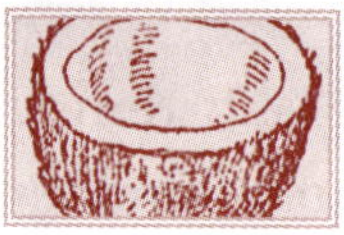

Preheat the convection oven to 400°F. Preheat a 12-inch skillet with an oven-proof handle or a 3 quart casserole in the oven. Combine the eggs, milk and the flour in a blender until well-blended. When the oven reaches 400°F, remove the pan and add 4 tablespoons butter to the pan to coat the bottom and sides. Pour the batter into the pan and return the pan to the oven. Bake 18 to 20 minutes until the edges are browned and crisp.

Peel and pit the mango and the papaya. Slice into ½-inch slices. In a skillet, melt the remaining 2 tablespoons butter and add the marmalade and the lemon juice. Add the fruit slices to the skillet and coat the fruit with the marmalade mixture. Stir just until the fruit is hot. Pour the fruit mixture into the browned puff pancake and top with the raspberries and flaked coconut. Serve immediately. Serves 6.

Wintertime Hot Fruit Compote

- 13 1/2 oz. pkg. sugar cookies, crumbled
- 16 oz. can sliced peaches, drained
- 15 1/4 oz. can pineapple chunks, drained
- 17 oz. can apricot halves, drained
- 16 oz. can pear halves, drained
- 21 oz. can cherry pie filling
- 1/2 c. pineapple juice

Sprinkle half of the sugar cookie crumbs into the bottom of a 2½ quart casserole. Layer the fruit on top of the cookie crumbs in the order in which they are listed. Pour the pineapple juice over all. Sprinkle with the remaining sugar cookie crumbs. Cover and refrigerate overnight.

Preheat the convection oven to 325°F. Remove the fruit from the refrigerator and let it sit for 30 minutes. Bake uncovered for 30 to 35 minutes or until the compote is bubbly. Serve immediately. Serves 8 to 10.

Ham & Eggs Breakfast Burritos

1 1/2 c. ham, chopped
1/4 c. onion, minced
3 T. butter, melted
12 eggs, lightly beaten
8 oz. Jack cheese, shredded
8 oz. cheddar cheese, shredded
3 T. milk
24 small flour tortillas

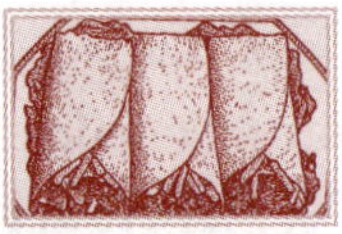

Grease or spray with a non-stick spray a 9" x 13" baking pan. Sauté the ham and onion in 1 tablespoon of the butter. Add the eggs and cook just until set. Add ½ of the Jack cheese and ½ of the cheddar cheese and stir slightly. Spoon this egg mixture into the tortillas and roll. Place the burritos seam side down in the prepared baking pan. Brush the tops with the remaining 2 tablespoons of the butter. Cover the pan with foil and seal tightly. Refrigerate overnight.

Preheat the convection oven to 325°F. Use a microwave oven to melt the remaining Jack cheese and cheddar cheese with 3 tablespoons of milk. Cook for about 1 minute on HIGH. Stir to blend. Cook for 1 minute or until the sauce is warm and smooth. Keep warm. Cover the burritos with aluminum foil and bake for 12 minutes covered with the foil, then another 12 minutes uncovered. Remove the burritos from the oven and top them with the cheese sauce. Serves 12.

Art's Favorite Rhubarb Brunch Cake

18 1/2 oz. pkg. yellow cake mix
1 c. water
1/3 c. vegetable oil
3 eggs
4 c. fresh or frozen rhubarb, sliced
1 c. sugar
2 c. whipping cream

Preheat the convection oven to 325°F. Grease and flour a 9" x 13" baking pan. In a large bowl, combine the cake mix, water, oil and the eggs with an electric mixer at low speed until moistened. Beat for 2 minutes on high. Pour the batter into the baking pan. Top the batter with the rhubarb and sprinkle with the sugar. Pour the whipping cream on top of the sugared rhubarb. Bake for 1 to 1¼ hours. Check for doneness by inserting a wooden pick into the center of the cake. If it comes out clean, the cake is finished. Serve warm. Refrigerate to store. Serves 12.

Maple Syrup Baked Pears

2 T. butter
4 large pears
1/2 c. pure maple syrup
1/2 t. ground cinnamon
1/2 c. walnuts, chopped

Preheat the convection oven to 325°F. Butter an 8" x 11" baking dish. Cut the pears in half, remove the core and the peel. Place the pears cut side down in the buttered baking dish. Pour the maple syrup over the pears and sprinkle them with the cinnamon. Bake uncovered for 25 minutes, or until the pears are tender when pierced with a fork. Sprinkle each pear with the walnut pieces. Serve warm. Serves 8.

Crunchy Cranberry Granola

- 6 c. regular oatmeal
- 1 c. shredded coconut
- 1 c. almonds, chopped
- 1 c. cashew pieces
- 1 c. dried cranberries
- 1 c. honey
- 1 c. water
- 1 c. canola oil
- 1 t. vanilla extract

In a large bowl, combine the oatmeal, coconut, almonds, cashews and cranberries. In a small bowl, combine the honey, water, canola oil and the vanilla. Add the honey mixture to the oatmeal mixture and combine thoroughly. Spread the mixture out on 2 ungreased baking sheets. Bake for 1½ hours, or until the granola is golden brown. Stir once during the baking process. Cool completely and store in an airtight container. Serves 10 to 12.

CHAPTER FOUR

Meats, Poultry & Seafood Main Dishes

The convection oven works most efficiently and superbly when cooking meats! In this chapter you will find recipes for outstanding beef, lamb and pork roasts, as well as recipes for roasted turkey and chicken. You will also find seafood recipes that produce tender, juicy fish. Some of the recipes that are included in this chapter are *Dijon Mustand & Honey Pork Roast, Fish Vera Cruz, Lamb with Kiwi & Port Sauce* and *French Scallop & Shrimp Pot Pie*.

If you are looking for a good hearty meal for the whole family, you'll want to try one of the casserole recipes in this chapter. The convection oven bakes casseroles thoroughly in less amount of time than a standard oven. The different flavors of a casserole bake together quickly and deeply to meld into a rich harmony. Try the *Swiss Cheese Chicken Noodle Bake,* or the *Shepherd's Pie*. Your children will enjoy the *Turkey Taco Bake* and the *Louisiana Pork & Beans.*

Any family-favorite recipe that you have on hand can be adapted for the convection oven. If the recipe calls for an oven temperature of 350°F, simply set the convection oven to 325°F. The timing will be about 25% less than the standard oven too, so adjust that as well.

Once you are comfortable with your convection oven, bake more than one dish at a time for that exceptional energy savings. For a large group of family and friends, two meat entrées create a delicious change of pace. Roast the *Farmhouse Roasted Turkey* for an hour in the convection oven and then add the *Elegant Lamb Roast* for the remainder of the baking time. These meats will roast superbly as the circulating hot air surrounds each piece. Enjoy the recipes from this chapter as you create entrées with extraordinary ease and flair.

Baked Pepperoni Rigatoni

- 8 oz. rigatoni pasta, cooked and drained
- 50 slices turkey pepperoni
- 1/2 c. parmesan cheese
- 1/2 c. onions, chopped
- 1/2 c. bell peppers, chopped
- 1 T. fresh basil, chopped
- 2 cloves garlic, minced
- 26 oz. prepared spaghetti sauce
- 2 c. mozzarella cheese, shredded

Preheat the convection oven to 350°F. Prepare a 9" x 13" pan with cooking spray. Layer one-half of the rigatoni, pepperoni, parmesan cheese, onions peppers, basil and garlic in the pan. Pour one-half of the spaghetti sauce over all. Sprinkle 1 cup of the mozzarella cheese over the spaghetti sauce. Layer the remaining pasta, pepperoni, parmesan cheese, onions, peppers, basil and garlic over the first half of the ingredients. Pour the remaining spaghetti sauce over and top with the remaining mozzarella cheese. Bake for 25 minutes, or until the cheese is melted and lightly browned. Serves 6 to 8.

Elegant Lamb Roast

- 4 to 5 lbs. leg of lamb, boned and rolled
- 3 T. prepared hot or sweet mustard
- 1/4 t. salt
- 3 T. butter
- 1 yellow onion, minced
- 1 carrot, sliced
- 2 celery stalks, sliced
- 1 to 2 c. water or lamb stock
- 1 T. all-purpose flour
- 2 to 4 T. sour cream
- 3 to 4 T. white wine

Spread all sides of the rolled roast with the mustard and then sprinkle with salt. Place the roast in a glass bowl, cover the bowl with foil and refrigerate for 1 day or overnight. Preheat the convection oven to 325°F. Heat the butter in a roasting pan over medium heat and brown the roast on all sides. Remove the roast from the pan and then brown the onion, carrots and the celery in the pan, about 3 to 4 minutes. Place the roast on top of the browned vegetables. Pour the water or lamb stock over the meat. Bake the roast 20 to 25 minutes per pound, approximately 1½ hours for a 4 pound roast. Baste the meat frequently as it bakes, adding more liquid if necessary.

When the meat is done, remove it to a warmed platter. Bring the pan juices to a boil on the stove and skim off any excess fat. Thicken the sauce with the flour. Stir in the sour cream until the sauce is smooth and season the sauce with the wine. Serve this sauce as an accompaniment to the roast. Serves 12 to 16.

Phyllo-Wrapped Chicken Breasts

- 3/4 c. mayonnaise
- 1/2 c. green onions, chopped
- 3 T. lemon juice
- 1 clove garlic, minced
- 1 t. dry tarragon
- 6 chicken breasts, boneless and skinless
- 12 sheets phyllo dough, thawed according to package directions
- 3/4 c. unsalted butter, melted
- 3 T. parmesan cheese, grated

Preheat the convection oven to 350°F. Combine the mayonnaise, green onion, lemon juice, garlic and the dry tarragon to make a sauce. Place a sheet of phyllo on your working surface. Keep a damp cloth over the remaining phyllo sheets. With a pastry brush, quickly brush melted butter over the first sheet. Place a second phyllo sheet on top of the first sheet, and brush with butter. Spread the sauce over all sides of 1 chicken breast. Place the breast in one corner of the buttered phyllo sheets. Fold the corner over the breast, fold the sides in over the breast, and then roll the breast up in the dough like a package. Place on an ungreased baking sheet. Repeat with the remaining chicken breasts.

Brush the 6 chicken breast packets with melted butter and sprinkle each with the parmesan cheese. These can be wrapped and sealed tightly and frozen, if desired. Thaw completely before baking. Bake in the convection oven for 20 to 25 minutes, or until golden. Serve hot. Serves 6.

Orange Glazed Ham

- 3 1/2 lb. ham, fully cooked and boneless
- 1/3 c. orange juice
- 3 T. honey
- 1 T. mustard
- 1/3 c. chicken broth
- 1 T. cornstarch
- 1/2 c. orange marmalade

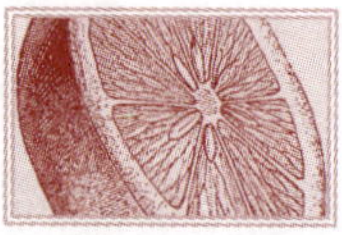

Combine 2 tablespoons of the orange juice, the honey and the mustard. Bring to boiling in a saucepan, stirring occasionally. Remove from the heat and cool the glaze to room temperature.

Make diagonal cuts about ¼-inch deep and 1 inch apart on the top of the ham. Place the ham on a rack in a shallow baking pan. Insert a meat thermometer into the center of the thickest portion of the meat. Bake in the convection oven at 325°F for approximately 1¼ hours, or until the thermometer registers 155°F. When the ham has baked for 45 minutes, brush the ham with half of the glaze sauce. Remove the ham from the oven, cover it with foil, and let it stand for 15 minutes. The temperature should rise to 160°F as the ham sits. Slice.

Mix the remaining orange juice, chicken broth and the cornstarch with the remaining glaze. Cook and stir until it is thick and bubbly. Stir in the marmalade and heat through. Pour the glaze into a serving pitcher and pass it with the sliced ham. Serves 12.

Dijon Mustard & Honey Pork Roast

3 lbs. pork loin roast, boneless
1 c. beer
1/2 c. honey
1/2 c. Dijon mustard
1/4 c. olive oil
1/2 yellow onion, chopped finely
1 clove garlic, minced
2 t. dried rosemary
1/2 t. salt
1/4 t. black pepper

Combine all of the above ingredients, except for the roast. Place the pork roast in a large plastic bag or plastic container. Pour the marinade over the roast and refrigerate for 4 hours or overnight.

Remove the pork roast from the marinade and reserve the marinade. Place the roast in a baking pan and bake in the convection oven at 325°F for 1½ hours, or until the meat is done when tested with a meat thermometer. Baste with the marinade occasionally.

Remove the roasted pork loin to a serving platter and slice. In a small saucepan, bring the remaining marinade to a boil. Reduce the heat and simmer for 10 minutes. Drizzle the marinade over the sliced roast to serve. Serves 10.

Lamb with Kiwi & Port Sauce

2 lb. lamb loin, boned
1 yellow onion, diced
1 clove garlic, minced
2 T. soy sauce
2 T. sesame oil
1 dash Worcestershire sauce
1 t. cracked pepper
2 to 4 kiwi fruits, sliced

Port Wine Sauce:
1 c. tawny port
1/4 c. chopped shallots
1 c. prepared brown sauce

Combine in a small bowl, the yellow onion, garlic, soy sauce, sesame oil, Worcestershire sauce and the cracked pepper. Rub the oil mixture over the lamb loin, place it in a plastic bag or glass container, and refrigerate overnight. One hour before cooking, remove the lamb from the refrigerator. Place the lamb loin in a baking pan and roast at 325°F for 1 hour, or until the meat is done when tested with a meat thermometer. The meat thermometer should read 140°F. Remove the meat and let it rest for 15 minutes. Slice the meat and serve it on a platter with the sliced kiwi. Accompany the meat and kiwi with the *Port Wine Sauce.*

Over medium heat, reduce the port from 1 cup to ½ cup. Add the shallots and heat through. Strain out the shallots, return the port to the heat, and add the brown sauce. Stir together completely and simmer for 5 minutes. Serve alongside the roasted lamb loin. Serves 4.

Garlic-Ginger Pork Roast

5 lbs. pork loin roast, boneless
1 T. ginger root, freshly grated
2 cloves garlic, minced
2 T. extra virgin olive oil
2 t. ground ginger
1 t. salt
1/2 t. black pepper
honey for basting

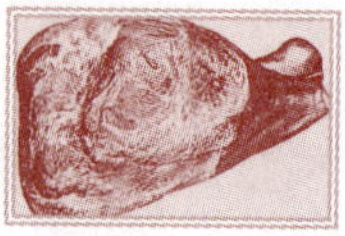

Run a sharp knife between the fat and the meat of the roast to form pockets. Using a long-bladed knife, insert the grated ginger into these pockets. In a small bowl, combine the garlic, olive oil, ground ginger, salt and pepper. Place the pork roast in a baking pan and brush with the oil mixture.

Bake the roast in the convection oven at 350°F for about 2½ hours, or 30 minutes a pound. Baste the meat every 30 minutes with the oil mixture as it roasts. During the last 15 minutes of baking, completely baste the roast with honey. Remove the meat from the oven and allow it to stand for 15 minutes before slicing. Serves 14.

Lamb and Feta Cheese Loaf

- 1/3 c. pine nuts
- 2 1/2 lbs. ground lamb
- 1 green pepper, diced
- 1 yellow onion, diced
- 3 cloves garlic, minced
- 2 eggs
- 2 t. black pepper
- 2 t. dried basil
- 1 t. dried rosemary
- 4 oz. crumbled feta cheese
- 8 oz. can tomato sauce

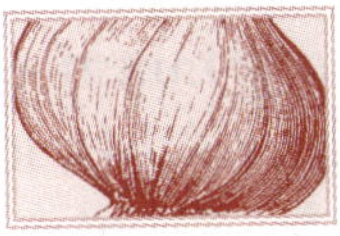

In a shallow pan, bake the pine nuts at 325°F for 5 minutes, stirring occasionally. Combine the pine nuts, ground lamb, green pepper, yellow onion, garlic, eggs, black pepper, dried basil and the dried rosemary. Press half of this meat mixture into a lightly greased 9" x 5" loaf pan. Sprinkle the top of this with the cheese. Press the remaining lamb mixture on top of the cheese and pour the tomato sauce over all. Increase the convection oven temperature to 350°F and bake the meat loaf for 1½ hours or until cooked completely through. Serves 8.

Manhattan Martini Pork Roast

2 lbs. pork loin roast, boneless
2 cloves garlic, minced
1/2 yellow onion, chopped
1/2 c. soy sauce
1/4 c. dry vermouth
1/4 t. black pepper

Stab the pork roast on all sides with a fork. Mix together the garlic, onion, soy sauce and the vermouth. Place the pork in a refrigerator container, pour the soy mixture over the meat, and then cover the meat with the black pepper. Refrigerate overnight. Preheat the convection oven to 325°F. Place the pork roast on a rack in a roasting pan and bake for approximately 1 hour, or until the meat thermometer shows 160°F. Remove the meat from the oven. Let it sit for 15 minutes and then slice and serve. Serves 4.

Sesame & Garlic Pork Tenderloin Medallions

1 1/2 lbs. pork tenderloin
4 T. soy sauce
2 T. sesame oil
2 T. brown sugar
1/2 t. honey
1 T. dry sherry
4 cloves garlic, minced
2 T. sesame seeds, toasted
3 to 4 scallions, diagonally sliced

Combine the soy sauce, sesame oil, brown sugar, honey, dry sherry, garlic, sesame seeds and the scallions. Pour this mixture over the pork tenderloin and marinate overnight. Remove the meat and discard the marinade. Bake the pork in the convection oven at 350°F for 45 minutes, or until the meat thermometer reads 160°F. Remove the tenderloin from the oven and slice it into medallions to serve. Serves 4.

Farmhouse Roasted Turkey

8 lbs. turkey
1 onion, cut into quarters
1 stalk celery, cut into quarters
1 carrot, cut into quarters
4 cloves garlic, cut in half
2 T. extra virgin olive oil
salt and pepper to taste

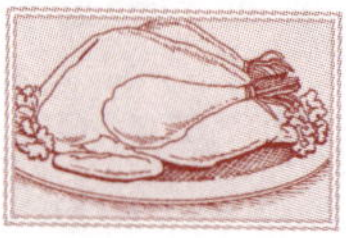

Remove the giblets from the cavity of the turkey. Rinse and dry the inside and outside of the turkey. Place the onion, celery and the carrot into the cavity. Sprinkle with salt and pepper. Pull the tail over the cavity and tuck the drumsticks under the band of skin, or truss the drumsticks closed. Twist the wing tips under the back. With a sharp knife, slide the blade between the skin and the meat, creating pockets. Place the garlic in these pockets. Place the turkey, breast side up on a rack in a shallow roasting pan. Rub the turkey with the olive oil and sprinkle with salt and pepper. Cover the turkey with foil. Roast in the convection oven at 325°F for 2½ to 3 hours. When completely cooked, the meat thermometer should read 180°F to 185°F. Remove the turkey from the oven and let it rest for 20 minutes. Discard the cavity vegetables and carve the meat to serve. Serves 8 to 10.

Savory Pork Spareribs

- 4 lbs. pork spareribs
- 12 oz. beer
- 1/2 c. honey
- 2 t. lemon juice
- 1 t. salt
- 1 t. dry mustard
- 1/4 t. black pepper

Cut the spareribs into 2-rib sections. Combine the beer, honey, lemon juice, salt, dry mustard and the ground black pepper. Put the ribs in a glass dish and pour the beer mixture over the meat. Marinate for 24 hours in the refrigerator. To bake, arrange the ribs in a single layer in a large baking pan. Bake in the convection oven at 325°F for 1½ hours, basting frequently with the marinade. Serve. Serves 4 to 6.

Beef & Barley Stuffed Peppers

- 3 large yellow, orange, red and/or green sweet peppers, halved lengthwise and seeded
- 1 lb. lean ground beef
- 1/3 c. green onions, sliced
- 1 c. barley, cooked
- 1 c. prepared chunky salsa
- 1/3 c. carrot, shredded
- 1/4 t. ground cumin
- 3/4 c. Jack cheese, shredded

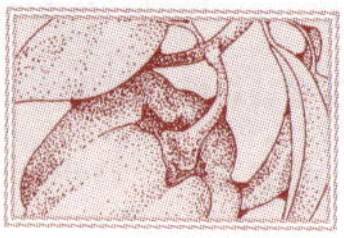

In a large saucepan, cook the pepper halves in boiling, salted water for 3 to 5 minutes, until just tender. Remove from the water and invert the pepper halves over paper towels to drain.

Preheat the convection oven to 325°F. In a skillet, brown the ground beef and green onions. Drain off the fat. Stir in the barley, salsa, carrot and the cumin. Mix well, then add ½ cup cheese and toss. Spoon the barley/beef mixture into the pepper halves and place them into a 9" x 13" baking pan. Bake, covered, in the convection oven for 20 minutes. Sprinkle the remaining cheese over the peppers and bake, uncovered, for another 5 to 10 minutes. The cheese should be melted when ready to serve. Serves 6.

Herbed Tenderloin of Beef

1 lb. tenderloin of beef, chine and silver skin removed
1 T. extra virgin olive oil
16 to 20 dried tomatoes
1 t. fresh thyme, minced
1 t. fresh basil, minced
1 t. fresh rosemary, minced
1 t. fresh parsley, minced
1 clove garlic, minced
1/4 c. parmesan cheese, grated
1/4 t. black pepper
1 t. kosher salt

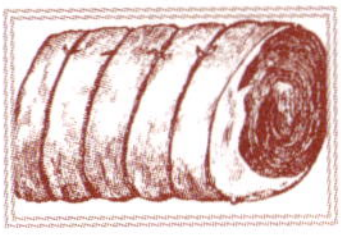

Preheat the convection oven to 350°F. After cleaning the tenderloin, split the roast down the middle and pound the meat out evenly. Rub with the olive oil. Lay the dried tomatoes evenly on the meat. Cover the tomatoes with the fresh herbs, garlic, parmesan cheese and the pepper and salt. Roll the meat and tie with unwaxed cotton cord for cooking.

Place the meat on a wire rack on a baking sheet. Bake for 15 minutes. The meat thermometer should read 140°F to 150°F for medium-rare. Let the meat stand for 15 minutes, then carve. Serves 4.

California Pesto & Three Cheese Pizza

Use homemade pizza dough or prepackaged pizza round.

Pesto:

1 c. extra virgin olive oil

2 c. fresh basil leaves

2 cloves garlic, minced

3 T. pine nuts

1/2 c. parmesan cheese, grated

Toppings:

1 onion, thinly sliced

1 sweet red pepper, sliced

1 green pepper, sliced

2 T. extra virgin olive oil

1 T. water

1/2 lb. garlic sausage

1/2 lb. sweet Italian sausage

2 T. cornmeal

1/4 c. goat cheese

3/4 c. mozzarella cheese, shredded

2 T. parmesan cheese, grated

Using a blender, combine the olive oil, basil, garlic and the pine nuts. Process until almost pureed. Stir in the cheese and set aside.

Sauté the onions and peppers over medium heat in one tablespoon of the olive oil and the water. When the peppers are soft, drain and set aside. Brown the sausages and drain off the excess fat. Coarsely chop the sausage. Preheat the convection oven to 375°F.

Spread the remaining oil over a 12-inch pizza pan and sprinkle the cornmeal over the oil. Place the pizza dough on the pan and flatten to the edges. Spread the pesto on the dough and then crumble the goat cheese evenly over the pesto. Add the onion, peppers, sausages and the cheeses. Bake 15 minutes or until the crust is slightly brown and the cheese is bubbly. Serves 4.

Swiss Cheese Chicken Noodle Bake

- 3 c. egg noodles
- 2 1/2 c. cooked chicken, chopped
- 1/2 c. onions, chopped
- 3 1/4 c. frozen broccoli cuts, thawed
- 10 3/4 oz. can cream of mushroom soup
- 1/2 c. milk
- 1/2 c. Swiss cheese, shredded
- 1 t. dried basil
- 1/2 t. salt
- 1/4 t. black pepper

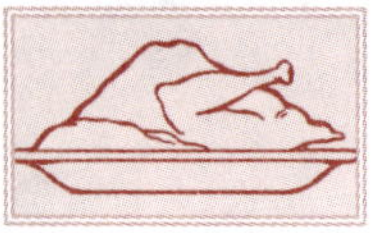

Preheat the convection oven to 325°F. Spray a 2½ quart casserole with cooking spray. Cook the noodles according to the package directions. Drain. In a mixing bowl, combine the noodles, chicken, onions and the broccoli. In another bowl, combine the soup, milk, cheese, basil, salt and the pepper. Stir the soup mixture into the noodle mixture. Pour the entire mixture into the baking dish. Bake, covered, for 40 minutes. Serves 6.

Chicken & Mushroom Rice

- 1 1/4 c. rice, uncooked
- 1 chicken, cleaned and cut into pieces
- 11 oz. can cream of celery soup
- 7 oz. can sliced mushrooms
- 1 c. water
- 1/2 c. white wine
- 2 T. butter
- 1 yellow onion, chopped
- 2 cloves garlic, minced
- 1/2 t. dried oregano
- 1/4 t. salt
- 1/4 t. black pepper

Preheat the convection oven to 325°F. Spray a 9" x 13" baking pan with cooking spray. Spread the rice evenly on the bottom of the pan. Layer the chicken pieces over the rice. In a mixing bowl, combine the cream of celery soup, mushrooms, water, wine, butter, onion, garlic, oregano and the salt and pepper. Pour this evenly over the chicken. Bake, covered, for 45 minutes. Remove the cover and bake for an additional 15 minutes to brown the chicken. Serves 6.

Southern Chili Cornbread Pie

- 1 lb. lean ground beef
- 1/2 c. onion, chopped
- 1/2 c. green pepper, chopped
- 15 1/2 oz. can chili beans in chili gravy
- 8 oz. can tomato sauce
- 6 oz. can tomato paste
- 1/2 t. chili powder
- 1/2 t. ground cumin
- 1/2 t. bottled hot pepper sauce
- 11 1/2 oz. pkg. refrigerated cornbread twists (10)
- 8 oz. dairy sour cream
- 2 T. all-purpose flour
- 1 c. cheddar cheese, shredded
- 2 c. corn chips, coarsely crushed

Preheat the convection oven to 350°F. In a large skillet, brown the ground beef, onion and the green pepper until the meat is no longer pink. Drain off the excess fat. Stir into the meat the undrained chili beans, tomato sauce, tomato paste, chili powder, ground cumin and the hot pepper sauce. Bring this to a boil. Reduce the heat and simmer uncovered for 5 minutes, stirring occasionally.

Lightly grease a 10-inch pie plate. Unwrap and separate the cornbread twists, but do not uncoil them. Arrange the twists in the pie plate, pressing them onto the bottom and up the sides of the plate. They will extend about ½-inch above the pie plate. Spoon the ground beef mixture into the crust. Combine the sour cream and the flour. Spread this on top of the beef mixture. Sprinkle with the cheese and the corn chips. Place the pie plate on a baking sheet. Bake, uncovered, for 20 minutes and then remove the pie from the heat. Let the pie stand for 10 minutes before serving. Serves 8.

Turkey Taco Bake

- 1 lb. ground turkey
- 1/2 c. yellow onion, chopped
- 1/2 c. green pepper, chopped
- 1 clove garlic, minced
- 1-oz. pkg. taco seasoning mix
- 1/2 c. prepared salsa
- 1 c. dairy sour cream
- 1 c. cottage cheese
- 1 c. tortilla chips, crushed
- 1 c. cheddar cheese, shredded

Preheat the convection oven to 375°F. Spray a 2 quart baking pan with cooking spray. In a skillet, brown the ground turkey, onions, peppers and the garlic. Add the seasoning mix and the salsa to the meat and mix well. In a medium bowl, stir together the sour cream and the cottage cheese. Place half of the crushed chips in the bottom of the baking pan. Add all of the meat mixture to cover the chips. Then cover the meat mixture with the sour cream mixture. Sprinkle with the cheddar cheese and top with the remaining crushed chips. Bake uncovered for 30 minutes. Serves 8.

Curried Cajun Chicken

1/3 c. honey
3 T. water
3 T. prepared mustard
2 T. butter, melted
2 t. Cajun seasoning
2 t. curry powder
1 t. lemon juice
1 clove garlic, minced
6 chicken breasts, halved, skinless, and boneless
hot, cooked rice

Preheat the convection oven to 325°F. In a 3 quart rectangular baking dish combine the honey, water, mustard, butter, Cajun seasoning, curry powder, lemon juice and the garlic. Mix well. Add the chicken breasts to the pan, turning to coat all sides, and then arrange in a single layer. Bake uncovered for about 30 minutes. Test the chicken with a meat thermometer before removing from the oven. Serve the chicken over the cooked rice. Serves 6.

Fish Vera Cruz

6 4 oz. fillets of a firm and mild fish (sea bass, red snapper, catfish)

1/8 t. salt

1/8 t. black pepper

2 T. butter

Vera Cruz Sauce:

1 T. extra virgin olive oil

4 cloves garlic, minced

1/2 c. yellow onion, finely chopped

2 lbs. tomatoes, peeled and finely chopped

1 green pepper, cut into strips

1/2 t. salt

1/4 t. black pepper

2 bay leaves

1 t. dried oregano

1/2 c. green olives, chopped

1/4 c. capers, drained

Twenty minutes before serving, preheat the convection oven to 350°F. Rinse the fillets and pat them dry. Season with salt and pepper. Melt the butter in a skillet and brown the fillets slightly on both sides. Transfer to a greased 9" x 13" baking pan.

Heat the oil in a large saucepan. Add the garlic and the onion and sauté for 3 minutes. Add the tomatoes and heat until the tomatoes are steaming and the juices are almost boiling. Stir in the green pepper, salt, pepper, bay leaves and dried oregano. Heat again, cover and cook on low for 8 minutes. Add the olives and the capers and remove the bay leaves. Spoon the *Vera Cruz Sauce* over the fish fillets, covering them completely. Bake, covered, for 10 to 15 minutes. Serve immediately. Serves 6.

Smoked Sausage & Gruyere Quiche

- 10 eggs
- 1 pt. heavy cream
- 1/2 t. salt
- 1/4 t. white pepper
- 1/8 t. dried basil
- 1/8 t. dried thyme
- 1/2 c. sliced smoked sausage or diced ham, fully cooked
- 1/4 c. green pepper, chopped
- 1/4 c. tomato, chopped
- 1/4 c. yellow onion, chopped
- 1/4 c. fresh mushrooms, sliced
- 2/3 c. Gruyere, Jarlsberg, or Swiss cheese, shredded

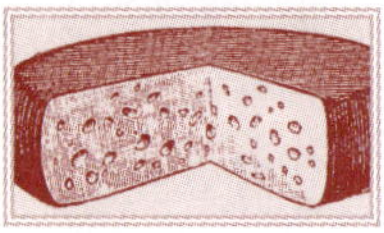

Preheat the convection oven to 325°F. Grease only the bottom of a 9 to10-inch quiche pan. In a medium bowl, mix the eggs, cream, salt, pepper, basil and the thyme until well-blended. In the prepared pan, lightly toss the meat, green pepper, tomato, onion and mushrooms. Sprinkle with the cheese. Pour the egg mixture over the meat mixture. Bake the quiche for 40 minutes or until golden brown. The quiche will be done when a knife inserted in the center comes out clean. Let the quiche stand for 10 minutes before serving. Serves 4 to 6.

Ham & Cheese Soufflé

1 loaf Italian bread, cubed	2 T. dry mustard
1 lb. cooked ham, cubed	8 eggs
12 oz. cheddar cheese, shredded	4 1/2 c. milk
6 T. all-purpose flour	1 t. salt
4 T. butter, melted	1 t. black pepper

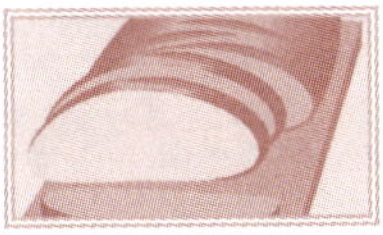

Spray two 2-quart casserole dishes with non-stick spray. Blend the bread, ham and cheese in a large mixing bowl. Distribute evenly into the two casserole dishes. In a mixing bowl, combine the flour, butter, dry mustard, eggs, milk and the salt and pepper thoroughly. Pour this egg mixture over the meat, distributing it evenly between the two casserole dishes. Stir and cover. Chill overnight. Bake uncovered at 325°F for 1 hour and 15 minutes. Serve immediately. Serves 12.

Tender Roast Beef with Spring Vegetables

3 lbs. beef round tip or eye round roast

1/4 t. salt

1/2 c. fresh parsley, chopped

1 T. extra virgin olive oil

5 cloves garlic, crushed

2 t. lemon peel, grated

1/2 t. black pepper

Vegetables:

1 T. extra virgin olive oil

1 lb. new red potatoes, halved

1/2 lb. carrots, cut in 1/2-inch diagonal slices

4 small yellow onions, halved

2 medium zucchini, cut in 3/4-inch slices

Preheat the convection oven to 325°F. In a large bowl, combine the salt, parsley, olive oil, garlic, lemon peel and the pepper. Reserve half of this seasoning mixture for the meat. With the remaining seasonings in the bowl, add 1 tablespoon of olive oil, blend well, and then add the vegetables. Toss to coat.

Press the reserved seasoning mixture onto the meat. Place the roast, fat side up, on a rack in a shallow roasting pan. Insert the meat thermometer in the thickest part of the roast. Arrange all of the vegetables around the meat, except the zucchini. Roast for approximately 1½ hours. The meat temperature should show 140°F for rare or 160°F for medium. Remove the meat and tent it with foil. Let the roast stand for 15 to 20 minutes.

Increase the convection oven temperature to 400°F, add the zucchini to the vegetables and continue roasting all of the vegetables for another 15 to 20 minutes. Slice the roast, remove to a platter and arrange the roasted vegetables around the meat to serve. Serves 8.

Classic Ham Tetrazzini

8 oz. mushrooms, sliced
1/2 c. onions, chopped
1 1/2 T. butter, melted
1/4 c. all-purpose flour
1/2 t. dry mustard
1 1/2 c. milk
1 c. hot water
1 chicken bouillon cube
8 oz. angel hair pasta, cooked and drained
2 c. cooked ham, diced
1/4 c. parmesan cheese

Preheat the convection oven to 325°F. Spray an 8" x 8" baking dish with cooking spray. In a skillet, sauté the mushrooms and onions in the butter until tender. Add the flour, mustard and milk. Dissolve the bouillon cube in the hot water and add to the onion mixture. Mix well. Boil until the sauce is thick and bubbly.

Pour the sauce over the cooked pasta, add the ham and mix well. Spoon the entire mixture into the baking dish. Sprinkle the top with the Parmesan cheese. Bake for 1 hour. Serves 8.

Tuscany Turkey Pasta

2 lbs. ground turkey
1 t. salt
1 1/2 oz. envelope spaghetti sauce mix
8 oz. can tomato sauce
6 oz. can tomato paste
1 1/2 c. water
10 oz. medium size shell macaroni, cooked and drained
16 oz. cottage cheese
1 1/2 c. cheddar cheese, shredded

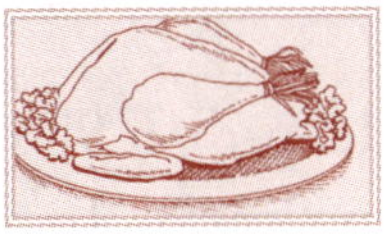

Preheat the convection oven to 325°F. Spray a 9" x 13" baking pan with cooking spray. In a large skillet, cook the turkey until it is no longer pink. Add the salt, spaghetti sauce, tomato sauce, tomato paste and the water. Mix well and bring to a boil. Simmer uncovered for 10 minutes, stirring occasionally.

Layer half of the shell macaroni in the baking pan. Layer half of the cottage cheese on top of the macaroni. Cover the cottage cheese with half of the meat sauce and sprinkle half of the cheddar cheese over the meat sauce. Repeat the layers ending with the cheddar cheese. Bake, uncovered, for 40 minutes in the convection oven. Serves 10.

Company Convection Oven Lasagna

- 3 16 oz. containers ricotta cheese
- 2 eggs
- 1 lb. mozzarella cheese, shredded
- 1/2 c. parmesan cheese, grated
- 1/2 c. fresh parsley, chopped
- 8 cloves garlic, minced
- 1/2 t. black pepper
- 2 lbs. lean ground beef
- 30 oz. jar spaghetti sauce
- 1 medium onion, chopped
- 1 green pepper, chopped
- 16 oz. box lasagna noodles, cooked and drained

Spray a lasagna pan or a deep-dish 9" x 13" baking pan with cooking spray. In a large bowl or food processor, combine the ricotta cheese, eggs, one-fourth of the mozzarella cheese, parmesan cheese, parsley, garlic and pepper. Blend to make a spreadable mixture. Add an extra egg, if needed, to make the correct consistency.

Preheat the convection oven to 325°F. In a skillet, brown the ground beef. Drain the excess fat. Add the spaghetti sauce, onion and the green pepper. Simmer 10 minutes. Spread 1 cup of the meat sauce over the bottom of the baking pan. Arrange one layer of lasagna noodles evenly over the meat. Cover the noodles with half of the ricotta cheese mixture.

Repeat the meat sauce, noodles and cheese layers. Sprinkle with the remaining mozzarella cheese. Cover the dish with foil. Bake for 45 minutes. Remove the foil and bake an additional 15 to 20 minutes. Remove from the oven and let stand for 15 minutes. Serves 12.

Southwestern Chicken

- 1 onion, chopped
- 1 T. extra virgin olive oil
- 3 ripe tomatoes, chopped
- 2 c. cooked chicken, cubed
- 1/2 c. chicken broth
- 2 t. ground chili powder
- 1/2 t. salt
- 1 t. dried oregano
- 1 t. dried cumin
- 6 small corn tortillas, cut into fourths
- 1 c. sharp cheddar cheese, shredded

Preheat the convection oven to 325°F. In a large saucepan, sauté the onion in the olive oil. Add the tomatoes, chicken, chicken broth, chili powder, salt, dried oregano and ground cumin. Bring to a boil. Reduce the heat and simmer for 5 minutes.

Spray a 9" x 13" baking pan with cooking spray. Layer half of the chicken mixture on the bottom of the pan. Cover the chicken with half of the tortillas, and then sprinkle with half of the cheese. Repeat the layers. Cover the pan with foil and bake for 25 minutes. Uncover and bake for 5 minutes. Serves 10.

Plum Tomato & Cilantro Pizza

4 small Italian flat breads
15 oz. can refried beans
2 c. Jack cheese, shredded
3 plum tomatoes, diced
1 green pepper, chopped
4 green onions, minced
1/2 c. fresh cilantro, chopped
2 cloves garlic, minced
1/4 c. prepared salsa
hot peppers (optional)

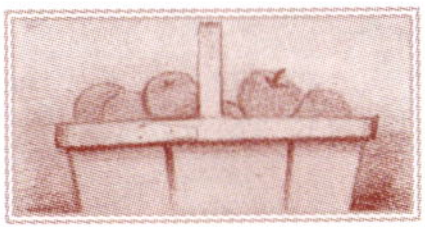

Preheat the convection oven to 400°F. Spread ¼ can of refried beans over each piece of Italian flat bread. Cover the beans with ½ cup Jack cheese. Top each pizza with tomatoes, green peppers, onions, cilantro and the garlic. Add the hot peppers, if desired. Bake the pizzas for 15 minutes. Drizzle the salsa over the top of each pizza and serve immediately. Serves 4.

Salmon, Dill & Shallot Quiche

- 6 oz. salmon fillet
- 2 T. white wine vinegar
- 1 bay leaf
- 5 peppercorns
- 1 T. fresh dill, finely chopped
- 2 T. fresh parsley, finely chopped
- 1 T. shallots, chopped
- 2 t. butter
- 3 eggs
- 1 c. half and half cream
- 1 1/2 t. Dijon mustard
- 1/4 t. salt
- 1 9-inch pie shell, baked
- 6 oz. cottage cheese
- 2 oz. sharp cheddar cheese, shredded

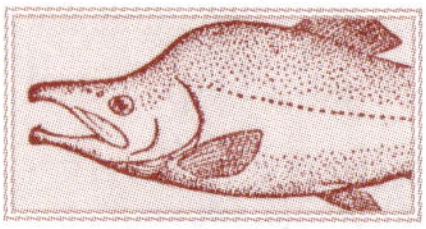

Preheat the convection oven to 425°F. Place the salmon in a shallow pan. Add just enough water to cover the fish. Season with the vinegar, bay leaf and the peppercorns. Poach gently on the stove, until the salmon tests done. Do not overcook.

Flake the salmon into ½-inch pieces and mix with the dill and parsley. Sauté the shallots in the butter until tender. Mix the shallots with the salmon and herbs. In a small bowl, beat the eggs with the half and half, mustard and the salt. Place the salmon mixture into the pie crust. Add the cottage cheese evenly over the salmon. Pour the egg mixture over all. Sprinkle the cheddar cheese on top.

Bake for 10 minutes. Reduce the heat to 325°F and bake until the filling is firm, about 20 minutes longer. Let the quiche rest for 10 minutes before serving. Serves 6.

Santa Fe Chili Pork Pie

- 1 1/3 c. chicken broth
- 3 medium potatoes, peeled and cut into 1/2-inch cubes
- 1 stalk celery, sliced
- 4 cloves garlic, minced
- 1 t. chili powder
- 1 t. ground cumin
- 1 t. ground coriander
- 1 t. dried oregano, crushed
- 1 t. dried thyme, crushed
- 1/4 t. celery salt
- 1 lb. boneless pork loin, cut into 1-inch cubes
- 2 T. vegetable oil
- 4 oz. can diced green chili peppers, drained
- 1/4 c. fresh cilantro, snipped
- 6 refrigerated biscuits

Preheat the convection oven to 425°F. Spray a 2-quart casserole with cooking spray. In a medium saucepan, combine the chicken broth, potatoes, celery and the garlic. Bring to a boil and simmer covered for 8 to 10 minutes. In a medium mixing bowl, combine the chili powder, cumin, coriander, oregano, thyme and the celery salt. Add the pork cubes and toss to coat. In a large skillet, sauté the pork in the vegetable oil until it is no longer pink. Drain off the excess fat. Add the potato mixture to the pork. Stir in the chili peppers and the cilantro. Bring to boiling. Pour this mixture into the prepared pan. Snip each biscuit into

4 pieces and arrange on top of the hot pork mixture. Bake uncovered for 15 minutes, or until the biscuits are golden. Cover with foil the last 5 minutes to prevent over-browning, if needed. Serves 6.

Louisiana Pork & Beans

- 1 3/4 lbs. pork shoulder roast, boneless and fat removed
- 1 T. vegetable oil
- 15 oz. can black beans
- 10 3/4 oz. can condensed cream of chicken soup
- 2 4 oz. cans diced green chili peppers, drained
- 1 c. quick-cooking brown rice
- 1/4 c. water
- 2 T. prepared salsa
- 1 t. ground cumin
- 1/2 c. cheddar cheese, shredded

Preheat the convection oven to 350°F. Spray a 2-quart casserole pan with cooking spray. Cut the pork into bite-size strips. In a large skillet, brown the pork until it is no longer pink. Drain off the excess fat. Stir in the black beans, cream of chicken soup, green chili peppers, brown rice, water, salsa and the cumin. Heat in the skillet until the mixture is just bubbly. Pour this mixture into the prepared pan. Bake uncovered for 25 minutes. Sprinkle with the cheese and bake 3 to 4 more minutes. Serves 6.

Shepherd's Pie

- 1 1/2 lbs. lean ground beef
- 1 c. yellow onion, chopped
- 2 cloves garlic, minced
- pinch dried thyme
- pinch savory
- 1/4 t. salt
- 1/4 t. black pepper
- 1/4 c. all-purpose flour
- 2 c. beef broth
- 1 t. Worcestershire sauce
- 2 medium carrots, diced small
- 4 large potatoes
- 3/4 c. milk
- 1 egg, lightly beaten

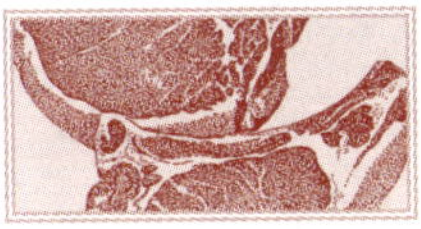

In a large skillet, brown the ground beef. Drain the excess fat. Add the onion and the garlic and cook until softened. Stir in the thyme, savory and the salt and pepper. Stir in the flour, broth, Worcestershire sauce and the carrots. Simmer about 20 minutes, or until the carrots are tender. Spread this meat mixture into a 10-cup baking dish. Cool slightly.

Preheat the convection oven to 375°F. Boil the potatoes until tender, then drain and mash. Beat in the milk and add half of the egg. Reserve the remainder of the egg. Spread the potato mixture over the meat mixture and brush with the remaining egg. Bake for 15 minutes until the top is golden brown. Serves 6.

French Scallop & Shrimp Pot Pie

- 1/2 c. dry white wine
- 1 lb. sea scallops, cut in half if large
- 1 large baking potato, peeled and cut into 1/2-inch cubes
- 3 T. butter, softened
- 1/2 c. tart apple, peeled and minced
- 1 large carrot, minced
- 1 stalk celery, minced
- 1 large onion, minced
- 1 clove garlic, minced
- 1 1/2 c. chicken broth
- 1/4 c. heavy cream
- 2 T. all-purpose flour
- 1/2 t. salt
- 1/2 t. white pepper
- pinch cayenne pepper
- 1 lb. medium shrimp, shelled and deveined
- 1 c. corn kernels
- 3 1/2 oz. jar pimento strips
- 2 T. fresh parsley, minced
- 1 9-inch pie crust

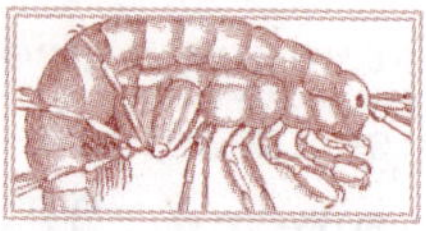

In a medium non-reactive saucepan, bring the wine to a boil over high heat. Add the scallops and cook until just opaque throughout, about 1 minute. Drain the scallops, reserving the liquid. In a saucepan of boiling water, cook the potato until just tender, 6 to 8 minutes. Drain and set aside.

Preheat the convection oven to 400°F. In a large saucepan, melt 2 tablespoons of the butter over medium heat. Add the apple, carrot, celery and onion and cook until the mixture softens, about 6 minutes.

Toss in the garlic and cook for 1 minute longer. Pour in the chicken broth and bring to boil. Boil this until most of the liquid has evaporated, about 5 minutes.

In a food processor, puree the apple mixture until smooth. Pour the puree back into the saucepan, add the reserved scallop liquid and the heavy cream. Bring this to a simmer over moderate heat and gradually add the flour, mixed with 1 tablespoon of the butter to make a paste. Bring to a boil, whisking until the mixture is thick and smooth. Reduce the heat to low, season with the salt, white pepper and the cayenne. Simmer about 2 to 3 minutes.

In a shallow 2-quart buttered baking dish, arrange the scallops in a single layer. Top with the shrimp and then the corn, potato and the pimento. Sprinkle the parsley over the top. Pour the sauce over all and gently shake the dish to distribute evenly. Roll out the pie crust a little larger than the dimensions of the baking dish. Place the dough over the top of the filled casserole dish and press against the outside rim to seal the edges. Cut several steam vents into the top of the crust. Bake the pot pie until the crust is golden brown, about 40 minutes. Serves 6.

Hot & Tangy Barbecued Ribs

- 4 lbs. pork ribs, cut in pieces
- 1 lemon, sliced
- 1 yellow onion, thinly sliced
- 1 c. catsup
- 1/3 c. Worcestershire sauce
- 1 t. chili powder
- 1 t. salt
- 2 dashes red pepper sauce
- 2 c. water

Preheat the convection oven to 425°F. Place the ribs in a shallow roasting pan, meaty side up. Layer the lemon and onion slices over the ribs. Roast for 30 minutes. In a saucepan, combine the catsup, Worcestershire sauce, chili powder, salt, red pepper sauce and water. Bring to a boil and cook for several minutes. Pour over the ribs and continue baking at 325°F for another 2 hours. Baste the ribs frequently while they are cooking. Serves 6.

Salmon with Hot Sweet Mustard

1 T. extra virgin olive oil	2 T. hot sweet mustard
4 lbs. salmon fillet	1 t. garlic, minced
1/4 c. mayonnaise	salt and pepper to taste

Preheat the convection oven to 325°F. Lightly oil a large shallow baking pan. Wipe the salmon with damp paper towels. Combine the mayonnaise, mustard, garlic and salt and pepper and spread it evenly on the salmon. Place the fish in the baking pan. Cover with aluminum foil. Bake for 15 minutes and then check for doneness. The fish is done when the meat flakes in the thickest part of the salmon. Serve immediately.

Serves 4 to 6.

Penne Pasta Bake

- 1 lb. ground beef or sausage
- 1 c. onion, chopped
- 1 clove garlic, minced
- 15 oz. can Italian style tomato sauce
- 14 1/2 oz. can diced tomatoes with herbs
- 6 oz. can tomato paste
- 1/2 c. water
- 12 oz. penne pasta, cooked and drained
- 4 c. mozzarella cheese

Preheat the convection oven to 325°F. Brown the meat, onion and the garlic in a skillet. Pour off any excess fat. Add the tomato sauce, undrained tomatoes, tomato paste and the water. Cook, stirring occasionally, for 10 minutes.

Layer half of the cooked pasta, half of the sauce and half of the cheese in a 9" x 13" baking pan. Repeat the layers. Cover and bake for 30 minutes until the casserole is bubbling and cooked through. Serves 8.

CHAPTER FIVE

Satisfying Vegetables & Accompaniments

Roasted vegetables provide the intense flavors of the good earth. In the convection oven these flavors deepen completely. The sugars of vegetables cook very quickly in the circulating hot air. This creates the sweet, crispy outer surface of the vegetables and locks in the richness of the deep vegetable flavor. Each bite brings enjoyment! Many recipes in this chapter combine vegetables with other ingredients to create a scrumptious ménage of flavors. *Irresistible Baked Beans, Parmesan Potato Gratin with Carrots, Cheesy Tomato and Squash Bake* and *Sweet Baked Onions* are a few of these wonderful combinations.

You will also find in this chapter recipes that can be used as the main entrée—*Walnut and Rice Stuffed Eggplant, Cheddar Cheese and Artichoke Frittata* and *Fresh Squash Ratatouille.* Each of these dishes provides an excellent source of nutritious ingredients along with rich flavors.

Add an earthy bread and seasonal fruit as accompaniments and you have a full meal! Try these recipes and add interest to your table and delight to your tastebuds.

Irresistible Baked Beans

64 oz. can seasoned baked beans, undrained
1/2 c. yellow onion, chopped
1/2 c. green pepper, chopped
1 clove garlic, minced
1/2 c. ketchup
1/4 c. honey
2 c. cheddar cheese, shredded
1/2 c. white, soft bread crumbs
1/2 t. salt
1/4 t. black pepper

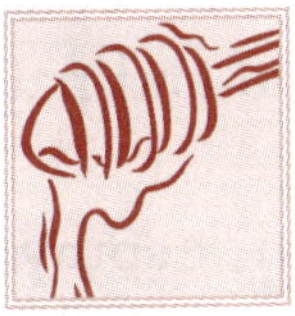

Preheat the convection oven to 325°F. Spray a 2 quart baking pan with cooking spray. In a mixing bowl, combine the beans, onion, green pepper, garlic, ketchup and honey. Mix well and spread this mixture into the pan. In a small bowl, combine the cheese, bread crumbs, salt and the pepper. Mix well and spoon over the bean mixture. Bake uncovered for 45 minutes, or until the top browns nicely. Serves 12.

Garlicky Roasted Potatoes

- 3 large russet potatoes
- 1/4 c. extra virgin olive oil
- 1/8 t. salt
- 1/8 t. black pepper
- 1/8 t. paprika
- 1 t. garlic salt with parsley (California-style)
- 2 T. parmesan cheese, grated

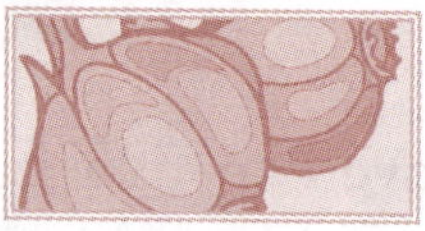

Peel the potatoes and cube into ½-inch pieces. Place them in cold water for 15 minutes, drain and pat dry. Preheat the convection oven to 400°F.

Spray a 9" x 13" baking pan with non-stick spray. Place the potatoes in the baking pan and toss with the olive oil to coat. Arrange in a single layer and sprinkle the potatoes with the salt, pepper, paprika, garlic salt and parmesan cheese. Bake for 25 minutes, turning the potatoes from time to time. Serve immediately. Serves 4.

Elegant Potatoes with Sour Cream Sauce

- 32 oz. frozen hash browns, thawed
- 1/2 c. onions, chopped
- 10 3/4 oz. can cream of mushroom soup
- 1/2 t. salt
- 1/4 t. black pepper
- 1 pint dairy sour cream
- 1 c. cheddar cheese
- 1/4 c. butter, melted
- 1 c. corn flake crumbs

Preheat the convection oven to 325°F. Spray a 9" x 13" baking pan with cooking spray. In a mixing bowl, combine the hash browns, onions, soup, salt, pepper, sour cream and cheese. Mix well. Spoon the mixture into the baking pan. In a small bowl, combine the butter and the corn flake crumbs. Sprinkle evenly over the top of the potato mixture. Bake the potatoes for 45 minutes, covered. Uncover and bake for 10 minutes, or until the potatoes are soft and cooked through. Serves 12.

Mushroom & Pepper Jack Cheese Quiche

Mushroom Quiche Crust:

1 lb. fresh mushrooms, coarsely chopped

3 T. butter or margarine

1/2 c. saltine cracker crumbs

1/8 t. salt

1/8 t. black pepper

6 to 8 green onions, chopped

2 T. butter or margarine

8 oz. Jack cheese, shredded

1 3/4 c. dairy sour cream

5 eggs

1/4 t. cayenne pepper

pinch paprika

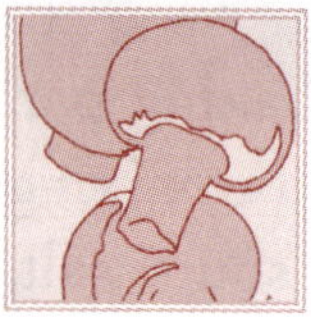

Preheat the convection oven to 375°F. In a skillet, sauté the mushrooms in the butter until they are soft. Stir in the cracker crumbs and the salt and pepper. Pat the mixture into a 10-inch pie pan that has been sprayed with cooking spray. Press the mushroom mixture evenly into the bottom and up the sides of the pan. Pat the mushroom mixture with paper towels to absorb any moisture.

Sauté the onions in the butter until soft. Spread the onions over the mushroom crust. Sprinkle the cheese over the onions. Beat together the sour cream, eggs and the cayenne pepper until the mixture is smooth. Pour this over the cheese and sprinkle with a touch of paprika for color. Bake for 30 to 35 minutes. Let the quiche rest for 10 minutes. Cut into wedges and serve immediately. Serves 8.

New Mexico White Corn Soufflé

8 eggs, lightly beaten
1/2 c. all-purpose flour
1 t. baking powder
3 t. dry mustard
2 c. cottage cheese
2 c. Jack cheese, shredded
2 c. cheddar cheese, shredded
2 c. frozen petite white corn
3 to 6 green chilies, chopped, peeled and roasted
1 t. paprika

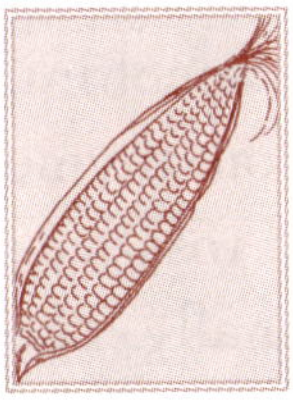

Preheat the convection oven to 325°F. Spray a 9" x 13" baking pan with cooking spray. Whisk the eggs with the flour, baking powder and the dry mustard. Stir in the cheeses, corn and the chilies. The batter will be lumpy. Pour this mixture into the baking pan. Sprinkle the top with paprika. Bake for 30 to 40 minutes. Check for doneness by inserting a sharp knife blade into the center of the soufflé. When the knife comes out clean, the dish is done. Serve this with warm flour tortillas. Serves 8.

Italian Roasted Balsamic Vegetables

- 1 small eggplant, sliced
- 1 medium zucchini, sliced
- 1 medium red onion, cut into small wedges
- 1 red bell pepper, thinly sliced
- 1 yellow bell pepper, thinly sliced
- 1 T. balsamic vinegar
- 1 T. extra virgin olive oil
- 1/2 t. dried thyme
- 1/4 t. black pepper

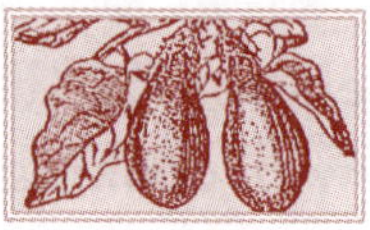

Preheat the convection oven to 400°F. Combine the eggplant, zucchini, onion, bell peppers, vinegar, oil, thyme and black pepper in a large baking dish and toss well to mix. Bake for 20 minutes, stirring occasionally. The vegetables should be just tender and very flavorful when done. Serves 4.

Green Chile Corn Quiche

9 eggs
1 T. butter
1 medium onion, finely chopped
13 3/4 oz. can artichoke bottoms, chopped
1/2 c. half and half cream
1/2 c. cheddar cheese, shredded
8 1/2 oz. can cream-style corn
4 oz. can diced green chilies
1/8 t. salt
1/8 t. pepper
1 10-inch prepared, unbaked pie crust

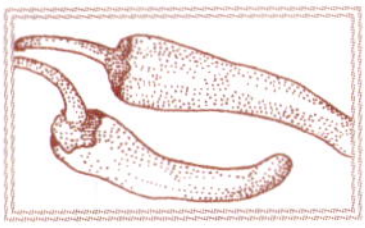

Preheat the convection oven to 350°F. In a large mixing bowl, beat the eggs until they are light yellow and slightly foamy. Sauté the onion in the butter until soft. Add the artichoke bottoms during the last few minutes. Pour the onions and the artichokes into the egg mixture and stir. Combine the remaining ingredients, except for the pie crust, into the egg mixture. Place the pie crust in a 10-inch quiche pan. Pour the egg mixture into the pie crust. Bake for 45 minutes or until the top of the quiche is nicely browned. Serve immediately. Serves 8.

Parmesan Potato Gratin with Carrots

4 T. unsalted butter
onion, thinly sliced
1 qt. heavy cream
2 c. milk
1 t. salt
1 t. black pepper
8 medium large potatoes, in 1/4-inch slices
6 medium large carrots, in 1/4-inch slices
3/4 c. parmesan cheese, grated

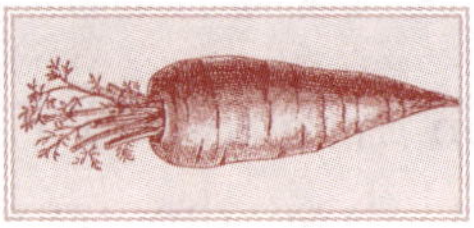

Preheat the convection oven to 350°F. Grease or spray with cooking spray a 9" x 13" baking pan. In a large saucepan over medium heat, melt 2 tablespoons of the butter. Add the onion and cook until the onion is translucent, about 5 minutes. Add the cream and the milk and bring it to a boil. Add the salt and pepper. Stir in the potato slices and the carrot slices, coating all of the vegetables well. Simmer the vegetables until the cream thickens and the vegetables are almost tender, about 8 minutes. Pour the vegetable mixture into the prepared baking pan and dot the top with the remaining butter. Sprinkle with the parmesan cheese. Bake uncovered for 10 to 15 minutes, or until the top is brown and the vegetables are tender. Serves 8 to 10.

Zesty Zucchini Frittata

4 medium zucchini, thinly sliced	1/2 t. garlic salt
6 eggs	1/4 t. ground black pepper
2 c. seasoned croutons	1/2 c. chopped onion
1 c. cheddar cheese	1 T. butter or margarine, melted

Arrange the zucchini on a steamer rack, cover and steam until the zucchini is tender, about 8 to 10 minutes. Spoon the zucchini into a bowl and mash. Pour the mashed zucchini through a strainer and let it sit for 5 minutes.

Preheat the convection oven to 325°F. Grease or spray with a cooking spray a 9" x 13" baking pan. In a large bowl, combine the strained zucchini and the eggs until well-blended. Stir in 1 cup of the croutons, the cheese, garlic salt, black pepper and the chopped onion. Pour into the prepared pan. Slightly crush the remaining 1 cup croutons and sprinkle them over the top. Drizzle with the melted butter. Bake, uncovered, for 15 to 20 minutes, or until the frittata is firm to the touch. Cut into large squares and serve hot. Serves 10 to 12.

Basil Asparagus with Portobello Mushrooms

- 4 lbs. asparagus, trimmed and peeled
- 1/2 lb. portobello mushrooms, cut into 1-inch chunks
- 3 T. extra virgin olive oil
- 1 t. salt
- 1/4 t. black pepper
- 2 sprigs fresh basil, coarsely chopped

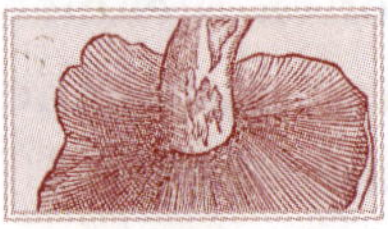

Preheat the convection oven to 425°F. On a baking sheet, toss the asparagus and the mushrooms with the olive oil, salt, black pepper and the basil. Spread the vegetables out in a single layer on the same baking sheet. Bake for 12 to 15 minutes, or until the vegetables are tender. Serve immediately. Serves 4 to 6.

Sweet Baked Onions

4 medium size sweet onions (Vidalia, Maui, etc.), peeled and cut in half

1/2 t. salt

1/4 t. black pepper

milk to cover onions

Butter a 9-inch baking pan. Place the onion halves in the baking pan in a single layer, cut side down. Sprinkle with the salt and black pepper. Pour just enough milk over the onions to cover them. Cover the baking pan with aluminum foil and seal tightly. Bake in the convection oven at 300°F for about 1¼ hours. When the onions are finished, the milk will be thickened and the onions will be sweetened by the concentrated roasting of the flavors. Serves 4 to 6.

Yams with Orange Sauce

- 6 medium sized yams, cooked, skinned and sliced
- 1 c. orange juice
- 1 T. cornstarch
- 3 T. butter, melted
- 1/3 c. packed brown sugar
- 1/3 c. sugar
- 2 T. corn syrup
- grated rind of 1/2 orange

Preheat the convection oven to 425°F. Grease or spray with cooking spray a 9" x 13" baking dish. Arrange the cooked yam slices in the dish. In a saucepan on medium heat, combine the orange juice, cornstarch, butter, sugars, corn syrup and the grated orange rind. Heat over medium, stirring constantly. When the sauce has thickened, pour it over the yam slices. Bake uncovered for 35 to 40 minutes. Serve warm. Serves 8.

Mushrooms, Green Peppers and Wild Rice

- 1 c. wild rice
- 3 c. water
- 2 T. butter or margarine
- 1/2 lb. mushrooms, chopped
- 1 green pepper, chopped
- 2 onions, chopped
- 2 c. tomato juice
- 1/2 c. parsley, chopped
- 1/4 t. paprika
- 1/4 t. thyme
- 1 t. salt
- 3/4 c. cheddar cheese, grated

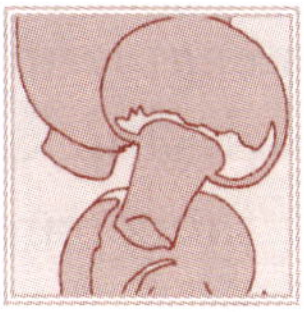

Cook the wild rice in the 3 cups of water for 20 minutes. Drain any excess liquid. Preheat the convection oven to 325°F. Grease or spray with cooking spray a 9" x 13" baking pan. In a large skillet, sauté in the butter the mushrooms, green peppers and the onions for 5 minutes. Add the tomato juice and cook for another 10 minutes. Add the parsley, paprika, thyme, and the salt. Stir to mix well.

In the baking pan, layer ½ of the rice. Cover the rice with ½ of the vegetable mixture and then sprinkle with ½ of the cheese. Repeat the layers. Bake covered for 35 to 40 minutes. Serves 8.

Walnut & Rice Stuffed Eggplant

4 eggplants, cleaned
1/2 c. onion, minced
1/2 c. mushrooms, chopped
1/4 c. walnuts, finely chopped
1 T. butter or margarine
1 c. cooked rice
3/4 c. cheddar cheese, shredded
2 eggs
1/4 c. seasoned bread crumbs
2 T. extra virgin olive oil
1 t. salt
1/4 t. black pepper

Cut 1 inch off the top of each eggplant and set aside. Hollow out each eggplant, leaving the sides about ½-inch thick. Steam the eggplants in a large saucepan for about 9 minutes. Remove and let them cool.

Grease or spray with cooking spray a baking pan that is large enough to hold all 4 eggplants. In a small skillet, sauté the onion, mushrooms and the walnuts in the butter until they are lightly browned. Mix together the rice, onion mixture, cheese, eggs and bread crumbs. Blend the olive oil, salt and pepper together with the rice mixture. Stuff each eggplant with the rice mixture and put the 1 inch piece of each eggplant back on top. Place the eggplants in the casserole. Bake at 375°F for 1 to 1½ hours. To serve, cut each eggplant in half lengthwise. Serve immediately. Serves 8.

Fresh Squash Ratatouille

1 medium zucchini, sliced

1 small eggplant, cut into 1/2-inch chunks

1 each yellow, red, and green bell pepper, thinly sliced

1 medium yellow squash, cut into 1/2-inch chunks

1 t. dry oregano leaves

1 T, dry basil leaves

3 T. extra virgin olive oil

1/2 t. salt

1/4 t. black pepper

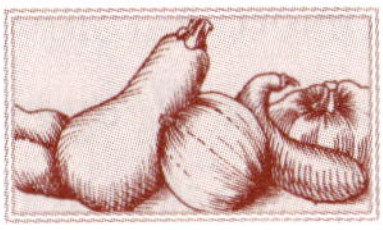

Preheat the convection oven to 400°F. Grease or spray with a cooking spray a 9" x 13" baking pan. Combine the zucchini, eggplant, bell peppers, yellow squash, oregano, basil, olive oil, salt and pepper. Mix well. Cover with aluminum foil and bake for 45 minutes, or until the vegetables are tender. Serve immediately. Serves 6.

Baked Parmesan Zucchini Sticks

2/3 c. parmesan cheese, grated
1/2 c. seasoned bread crumbs
1 T. dried parsley
2 large eggs
5 medium size zucchini, ends trimmed
1 T. extra virgin olive oil
1/2 t. salt

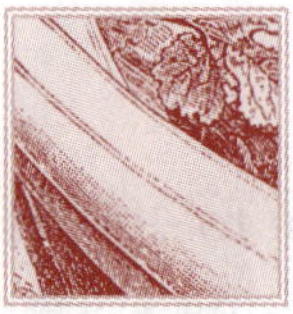

Preheat the convection oven to 425°F. In a small bowl, combine the parmesan cheese, bread crumbs and dried parsley. In another small bowl, beat the 2 eggs completely. Cut each zucchini in half lengthwise, then in half lengthwise again. Dip each zucchini stick into the eggs and then roll it in the bread crumb mixture to cover. Place the coated zucchini sticks in a single layer on a baking sheet that has been coated with cooking spray. Drizzle the sticks with olive oil. Bake for 18 to 20 minutes, or until the zucchini sticks are golden brown and crusty. Remove from the oven and sprinkle with salt. Serve immediately. Serves 6.

Cheesy Tomato and Squash Bake

- 2 T. butter, melted
- 1 small onion, sliced into rings
- 4 small zucchini, in 1-inch slices
- 4 small yellow squash, in 1-inch slices
- 14 1/2 oz. can whole tomatoes, undrained
- 1/4 t. salt
- 1/4 t. black pepper
- 1/4 c. parmesan cheese

Preheat the convection oven to 325°F. Sauté the onion rings and the squash in the melted butter just until they become warm. Pour the squash mixture into a large baking pan. Add the canned tomatoes and the salt and pepper. Stir well. Bake covered for 10 minutes. Remove the cover and continue baking for another 15 minutes, or until the vegetables are lightly browned and heated through. Sprinkle with the parmesan cheese and serve immediately. Serves 4.

Mexican Corn & Swiss Cheese

- 16 oz. can Mexican corn with peppers
- 15 1/2-oz. can evaporated milk
- 1 egg, beaten
- 2 T. onion, chopped
- 1/2 t. salt
- 1/4 t. black pepper
- 1 c. Swiss cheese, shredded
- 1/2 c. soft bread crumbs
- 1 T. butter, melted

Preheat the convection oven to 325°F. Grease or spray with cooking spray a 2-quart baking pan. Combine the corn, evaporated milk, beaten egg, onion, salt, pepper and ¾ cup of the Swiss cheese. Pour the mixture into the casserole dish. Toss the bread crumbs with the butter and remaining cheese. Sprinkle this over the top of the corn mixture. Bake for 20 to 25 minutes. Serve immediately. Serves 6.

Cheddar Cheese and Artichoke Frittata

- 1 c. water-packed artichoke hearts, drained
- 1/4 c. onion, finely chopped
- 1 c. cheddar cheese, shredded
- 6 eggs
- 1/4 c. half and half cream
- 1/4 c. milk
- 1/4 t. salt
- 1/8 t. black pepper
- 1 T. fresh parsley, chopped
- 1/4 c. parmesan cheese, grated

Preheat the convection oven to 325°F. Grease or spray with cooking spray a 9-inch square baking pan. Spread the artichoke hearts in the pan. Top the hearts with the onion and the cheese. Beat together the eggs, half and half, milk, salt, pepper and parsley. Pour the egg mixture over the top of the cheese. Sprinkle the egg mixture with the parmesan cheese. Bake for 15 to 20 minutes, or until the frittata is puffy and lightly browned. The center of the frittata will feel firm. Serve immediately. Serves 4 to 6.

CHAPTER SIX

Delightful Bakery Breads, Muffins and Rolls

One of the enjoyments of baking is the aroma that wafts through the kitchen into the rest of the home. There is nothing like the smell of baking breads, muffins or rolls! If the bread is a yeast dough, the fragrance is even more enticing. It conjures up the comfort of home and the warmth of a family.

Some of the recipes in this chapter are quick breads like *Lemon Tea Bread, Summer Harvest Zucchini Bread* and *Buttery Spice 'n' Pecan Muffins*. The recipe for *Buttery Irish Scones* is also quick and easy. These scones bake to a rich tenderness for a morning breakfast. The *Bakery Banana Muffins, Homestyle Blueberry Muffins* and *Oatmeal Cinnamon Muffins* are tried and true favorites for the whole family.

If you are ready to bake some yeast breads, you will find included in this chapter *English Muffin Bread, Gingered*

Yeast Rolls and *Rosette Dinner Rolls*. These can be prepared and served when a more elegant type of bread is desired. The *Sicilian Pesto Biscuits* and *Rosemary Foccacia* are perfect as an accompaniment for the light lunch or dinner.

All of these wonderful recipes will bake to a flawless finish in the convection oven. As the hot air circulates around and between these bakery goods, the dough rises, the golden crust forms and the inside of the baked food is beautifully moist and tender. You will find satisfaction as you bake and serve these breads to your family and friends!

Oatmeal Cinnamon Muffins

- 1 c. old-fashioned oats
- 1 c. buttermilk
- 2 eggs, lightly beaten
- 1 c. all-purpose flour
- 1/3 c. packed brown sugar
- 1 1/2 t. baking powder
- 1 t. ground cinnamon
- 1/2 t. baking soda

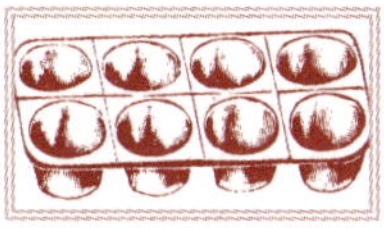

Preheat the convection oven to 375°F. In a large bowl, combine the oats and buttermilk. Let this stand for 5 minutes, then stir in the eggs. In a separate bowl, combine the flour, brown sugar, baking powder, cinnamon and baking soda. Stir this into the oatmeal mixture just until moistened. Fill greased or paper-lined muffin cups two-thirds full. Bake for 18 to 20 minutes, or until the muffins are done. Cool in the pan for 10 minutes before removing to a wire rack to cool. Serve warm. Makes 8 to 10 muffins.

Buttery Spice 'n' Pecan Muffins

1 c. butter or margarine, softened
2 c. sugar
2 eggs
2 c. unsweetened applesauce
1 t. ground cloves
2 t. ground allspice
3 t. ground cinnamon
1 t. salt
2 t. baking soda
4 c. all-purpose flour
1 1/2 c. pecans, chopped
cinnamon-sugar (1/2 cup sugar mixed with 1/2 t. cinnamon)

Preheat the convection oven to 325°F. Cream together the butter and the sugar. Add the eggs, one at a time. Mix in the applesauce and the spices. Sift together the salt, baking soda and the flour. Add to the applesauce mixture and mix well. Stir in the pecans. Pour the batter into muffin tins that have been sprayed with cooking spray. Sprinkle the cinnamon-sugar over the top of the muffin batter and bake for 25 minutes. Let the muffins cool for 10 minutes and then remove from the muffin pan. Serve warm. Makes 3 to 4 dozen muffins.

Bakery Banana Muffins

- 2 1/2 c. all-purpose flour
- 3/4 c. sugar
- 1 T. double acting baking powder
- 1/2 t. salt
- 6 T. butter or margarine
- 3 ripe bananas, cut into quarters
- 2 eggs
- 1/3 c. milk
- 1 t. vanilla extract

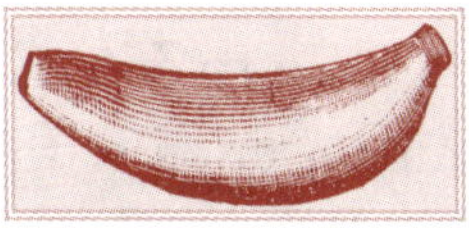

Preheat the convection oven to 375°F. Grease or spray 12-18 muffin cups with cooking spray. In a large bowl, combine the flour, sugar, baking powder and the salt. With a pastry blender, cut in the butter until the mixture resembles coarse crumbs. Set aside.

In a covered blender, combine the bananas, eggs, milk and the vanilla just until the bananas are chopped. Stir the banana mixture into the flour mixture until moistened. Spoon the batter into the muffin cups. Bake for 20 to 25 minutes. Remove from the oven and serve warm. Makes 12 to 18 muffins.

Homestyle Blueberry Muffins

1 3/4 c. all-purpose flour
1/2 c. sugar
3 t. baking powder
1/2 t. salt
1 c. frozen blueberries, thawed, rinsed and drained
1 c. milk
1/2 c. butter, melted
1 egg

Preheat the convection oven to 350°F. Grease or spray 12 muffin cups with cooking spray. Stir together the flour, sugar, baking powder and the salt. Add the frozen blueberries and stir until they are coated with the flour mixture. In a separate bowl, combine the milk, butter and the egg. Add this egg mixture to the flour mixture and stir just until moistened. Do not beat. Pour the batter into the muffin cups and bake for 20 minutes. Remove from the oven and serve warm.
Makes 12 muffins.

Gingered Yeast Rolls

1/2 c. milk
2 T. butter
2 T. sugar
1/2 t. salt
1 T. active dry yeast
3 1/4 c. bread flour
1/4 t. ground ginger

Grease or spray 12 muffin cups with cooking spray. Heat the milk, butter and the sugar in a medium saucepan until the butter is melted and the milk is warm. Set aside to cool in a large mixing bowl. When the milk mixture has cooled to 120°F, add the yeast, 3 cups of the flour and the ginger. Combine to form a soft dough, adding additional flour if needed to prevent stickiness. Cover the dough and let it rest for 10 minutes.

Turn the dough out on a floured surface and shape into a long roll. Divide it into 12 equal-sized pieces. Shape these into balls using the palms of the hands. Place the balls of dough into the muffin cups; cover, and let the dough rise until it has doubled, about 1½ to 2 hours.

Preheat the convection oven to 375°F. Bake the rolls for 18 to 20 minutes or until they are nicely browned. Remove from the oven and cool for 5 minutes. Serve warm. Makes 12 rolls.

Rosette Dinner Rolls

4 c. all-purpose flour
1/4 oz. pkg. active dry yeast
1 c. milk
1/4 c. sugar
1/4 c. butter or margarine
1/2 t. salt
3 egg yolks
1 egg yolk, slightly beaten
1 T. water

In a large mixing bowl, combine 1½ cups of the flour and the yeast. In a medium saucepan, heat and stir the milk, sugar, butter and the salt until the butter is almost melted and the milk is warmed (115-120°F). Add the warm milk mixture to the flour mixture and stir. Add the 3 egg yolks and beat with an electric mixer on low speed for 30 seconds. Scrape the sides of the bowl clean and then beat on high speed for 3 minutes. Stir in as much of the remaining flour as possible, one cup at a time.

On a lightly floured surface, knead in enough of the remaining flour to make a moderately stiff dough. Knead for 6 to 8 minutes until the dough becomes elastic. Shape the dough into a ball, place it into a greased bowl, and turn once. Cover and let the dough rise until it is double, about 1½ to 2 hours.

Punch the dough down, turn it out onto a lightly floured surface and divide in half. Divide each half into 12 pieces. Cover and let these pieces rest for 10 minutes. Meanwhile grease or coat with cooking spray 2 baking sheets. To assemble the rosettes, roll each piece of dough into a 12-inch rope. Tie the rope into a loose knot. Tuck the ends of the rope underneath the body of the knot, making a dinner roll that resembles a flower. Place these rolls, spaced 3 inches apart, on the baking sheets. Cover and let rise in a warm place until nearly double, about 30 minutes.

Preheat the convection oven to 350°F. Mix together the slightly beaten egg yolk and the tablespoon of water. Brush the tops of the rolls with this egg wash. Bake for 10 to 12 minutes, until the tops are golden. Remove the rolls from the baking sheet and cool on a wire rack. Serve warm with softened butter.

These rolls can be made and frozen. After cooling, place them in a single layer in a freezer container or bag and freeze for up to 3 months. Before serving, thaw at room temperature for about 2 hours. Makes 24 rolls.

Doubly Decadent Muffins

1/2 c. butter or margarine, melted	1/2 c. peanut butter chips
1/2 c. brown sugar	1/4 c. walnuts, chopped
1 t. vanilla extract	1/4 c. pecans, chopped
2/3 c. milk	1/2 t. salt
2 eggs	1 t. baking powder
1/2 c. chocolate chips	2 1/4 c. all-purpose flour

Preheat the convection oven to 350°F. Grease or spray 12-18 muffin cups with cooking spray. Combine the butter, brown sugar, vanilla, milk and the eggs. Add the chips and the nuts and blend with the moist ingredients. In a separate bowl, combine the salt, baking powder and the flour. Add this to the milk mixture, stirring just until the dry ingredients are moistened. Fill the muffin cups with the batter and bake for 15 to 20 minutes. Remove the muffins from the oven, cool, and serve. Makes 12 to 18 muffins.

Lemon Zest Muffins

1 3/4 c. all-purpose flour	2/3 c. milk
1/2 c. sugar	1 T. lemon zest
1 T. baking powder	1 T. lemon juice
1/2 t. salt	1/3 c. vegetable oil
1 egg	3 T. sugar

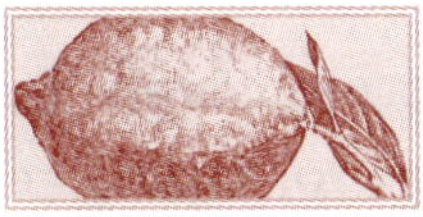

Preheat the convection oven to 350°F. Grease or spray 12 muffin cups with cooking spray. Combine the flour, ½ cup sugar, baking powder and the salt in a medium bowl. In a small bowl, beat the egg lightly. Add the milk, 2½ teaspoons of the lemon zest, the lemon juice and the oil. Add the liquid to the flour mixture and stir just until moistened. Spoon the batter into the muffin cups.

Combine the remaining 3 tablespoons sugar and the ½ teaspoon lemon zest. Sprinkle this over the tops of the muffins. Bake for 20 minutes. Serve warm. Makes 12 muffins.

Buttery Irish Scones

2 c. all-purpose flour
1/3 c. sugar
2 t. baking powder
1/8 t. salt
1/3 c. chilled unsalted butter
1 egg, beaten
1 t. vanilla
1/2 c. whipping cream

1 egg, well-beaten
1 T. heavy cream

Preheat the convection oven to 350°F. Lightly grease or spray a baking sheet with cooking spray. In a large bowl, combine the flour, sugar, baking powder and the salt. With a pastry blender, cut the butter into the flour mixture until it resembles coarse crumbs. In a small bowl, combine the beaten egg, vanilla and the whipping cream. Add this mixture to the flour mixture. Stir just until combined. Do not overmix.

On a lightly floured surface, knead the dough gently. Pat the dough into a 7-inch circle that is 1½-inch thick. Cut this circle into 8 triangles, or use a biscuit cutter to make rounds. Place the scones onto the baking sheet. Mix together the well-beaten egg and the tablespoon of heavy cream and brush over the tops of the scones. Bake for 12 to 15 minutes, until the scones are lightly browned. Serve warm. Makes 8 scones.

(Variations to these scones can be the addition of ½ cup dried fruit and/or nuts. Add these to the flour mixture, before adding the liquid ingredients. Nuts can also be sprinkled on the top of the scones after they have been brushed with the egg mixture. These scones freeze well.)

Sicilian Pesto Biscuits

- 2 c. all-purpose flour
- 3 T. buttermilk powder or nonfat dry milk powder
- 2 t. baking powder
- 1/2 t. baking soda
- 1/4 t. salt
- 1/3 c. shortening
- 2 T. prepared pesto
- 2/3 c. water

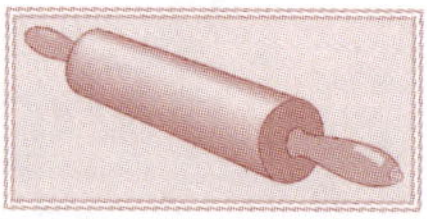

Preheat the convection oven to 400°F. In a large bowl, stir together the flour, buttermilk or milk powder, baking powder, baking soda and the salt. With a pastry cutter, cut in the shortening and the pesto until the mixture resembles coarse crumbs. Make a well in the center of the mixture and add the water all at once. Stir just until the dough clings together.

Turn the dough out onto a lightly floured surface. Knead gently for 10 to 12 strokes. Roll or pat the dough to ½-inch thickness. Cut with a lightly floured 2½-inch biscuit cutter. Place the biscuits on an ungreased baking sheet. Bake for 8 to 10 minutes or until the biscuits are golden. Makes 10 to 12 biscuits.

English Muffin Bread

- 5 to 6 c. flour
- 1/2 c. seedless raisins, optional
- 2 1/4 oz. pkgs. of active dry yeast
- 1 T. sugar
- 2 t. salt
- 1 1/2 t. ground cinnamon
- 1/4 t. baking soda
- 2 c. milk
- 1/2 c. water
- cornmeal

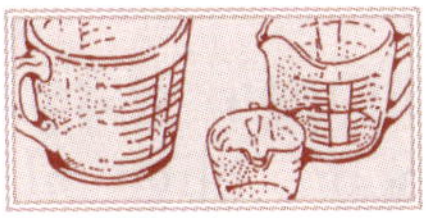

In a large bowl, combine 3 cups flour, raisins, yeast, sugar, salt, cinnamon and the baking soda. Combine the milk and the water in a pan and heat until the milk is very warm, 120°F to 130°F. Add the milk mixture to the dry ingredients and beat well. Stir in the remaining flour to make a stiff batter.

Grease two 9" x 5" loaf pans and coat them with cornmeal. Divide the batter into the two loaf pans. Sprinkle the tops of the loaves with additional cornmeal. Cover and let the bread rise for 45 minutes. Preheat the convection oven to 375°F. Place the 2 pans into the oven and bake for 20 to 25 minutes, until the bread is brown and hollow-sounding. Remove the bread from the pans immediately and cool. Slice and toast and serve. Makes 2 loaves.

Rosemary Focaccia

2 pkgs. fast-rising dry active yeast
2 c. tepid water (105°F-110°F)
2 T. sugar
4 T. extra virgin olive oil
1/2 c. vegetable oil
1 t. salt
5 1/2 c. all-purpose flour
3 cloves garlic, crushed
1/4 c. extra virgin olive oil
1 T. fresh rosemary, minced
1 T. kosher salt

Dissolve the yeast in the tepid water. Add the sugar, 4 tablespoons olive oil, vegetable oil and the table salt. Mix in 3 cups of flour and whip until the dough begins to leave the sides of the mixing bowl, about 10 minutes. Mix in the remaining flour by hand and knead the dough until it is smooth. Place the dough in a greased bowl, turning once. Cover and let the dough rise until it is doubled, about 1½ to 2 hours. Punch the dough down and then allow it to rise again.

Lightly oil two baking sheets. Divide the dough in half and place each half on a sheet. Using your fingers, press the dough out to the edges of the pan. Cover the dough and allow it to rise for 30 minutes. Preheat the convection oven to 325°F. Mix together the ¼ cup of olive oil and the garlic. Brush this mixture over the top of the breads. Sprinkle with the rosemary and the kosher salt. Bake for 30 minutes. Remove the breads from the oven and place on cooling racks. Serve warm or cold. Makes 2 loaves.

Lemon Tea Bread

8 oz. cream cheese, softened
1/2 c. butter or margarine, softened
1 1/4 c. sugar
2 eggs
2 1/4 c. all-purpose flour
1 T. baking powder
1/2 t. salt
3/4 c. milk
1 T. lemon rind, grated
2/3 c. blanched almonds, toasted and finely chopped
2/3 c. powdered sugar, sifted
2 T. lemon juice

Preheat the convection oven to 325°F. Grease and flour two 9" x 5" loaf pans. In a large bowl, beat the cream cheese and butter with an electric mixer at high speed, until light and fluffy. Gradually add the sugar, beating well. Add the eggs, one at a time, beating after each egg.

In a medium bowl, combine the flour, baking powder and the salt. Alternately add the flour mixture and the milk into the egg mixture, mixing well after each addition. Stir in 2 teaspoons of the lemon rind and all of the almonds. Pour the batter into the two loaf pans. Bake for 45 minutes until a wooden pick inserted in the middle of the bread comes out clean.

Combine the remaining 1 teaspoon lemon rind with the powdered sugar and the lemon juice. Stir well. Spoon this glaze over the warm loaves. Let the bread cool in the pans for 10 minutes and then remove to a wire rack. Makes 2 loaves.

Summer Harvest Zucchini Bread

- 2 c. sugar
- 3 eggs
- 3/4 c. vegetable oil
- 2 t. vanilla extract
- 2 c. zucchini, grated
- 3 c. all-purpose flour
- 1 T. baking powder
- 1 t. baking soda
- 2 t. ground cinnamon
- 1/2 t. ground nutmeg
- 1/2 t. ground allspice
- 1 c. crushed pineapple, drained
- 1 c. walnuts or pecans, chopped
- 1 c. raisins, optional

Preheat the convection oven to 325°F. Grease and flour 3 9" x 5" loaf pans. In a large mixing bowl combine the sugar, eggs, oil and the vanilla. Mix well. Stir in the grated zucchini. In a separate bowl, combine the flour, baking powder, baking soda, cinnamon, nutmeg and the allspice. Add the flour mixture to the zucchini mixture and combine well. Stir in the crushed pineapple, nuts and raisins. Divide the dough evenly between the 3 loaf pans. Bake for 1 hour. Let the breads cool in the pans for 10 minutes and then remove to a wire rack. Makes 3 loaves.

CHAPTER SEVEN

Luscious Convection Oven Desserts

Delectable desserts can be the finale for a fine meal and the center of attention for great occasions. They also remind us of childhood, home and holidays. The convection oven bakes all of these wonderful treats beautifully. Your special cake, pie and soufflé will bake to a glorious finish and your favorite desserts will come out perfectly. Within this chapter, you will find many different types of desserts. Some of them are elegant and others are those favorites that comfort our hearts and souls. Those special desserts include *Sour Cream Blintz Soufflé, Raisin Bread Pudding with Hard Sauce,* and *Chocolate Kahlúa® Cake*. These might involve some extra time in preparing but they finish as gorgeous desserts that bring "oohs" and "aahs" from your family and guests.

For those old-time favorites, this chapter has *Old-Fashioned Peanut Butter Cookies, Favorite Chocolate Chip Oatmeal Cookies* and *Heartwarming Blackberry Cobbler*. The

Fresh Strawberry Shortcake is a sheer delight for summertime. And, try the *Cappuccino Tarts* for a unique afternoon respite. All of these scrumptious desserts await flawless baking in your convection oven. You and those you love will enjoy the end results of the recipes in this chapter!

Sour Cream Blintz Soufflé

Batter:
1/2 c. butter, softened
1/3 c. sugar
6 eggs
1 c. all-purpose flour
2 t. baking powder
1 1/2 c. dairy sour cream
1/2 c. orange juice

Filling:
18 oz. cream cheese, softened
1 pt. ricotta cheese
1 T. sugar
1 t. vanilla extract
2 egg yolks

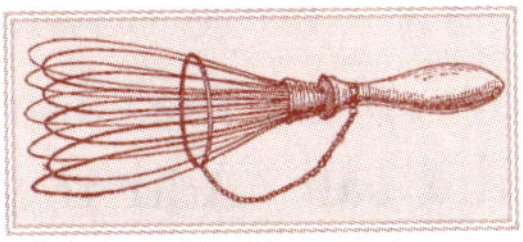

Preheat the convection oven to 325°F. In a large bowl, cream the butter and the sugar. Add the eggs and beat well. In a separate bowl, combine the flour and the baking powder. Add the flour mixture alternately with the sour cream and the orange juice to the egg mixture. Stir just until moistened. Pour half of this batter into a buttered 9" x 13" baking dish.

In a medium bowl, beat the cream cheese until smooth. Add the ricotta cheese, sugar, vanilla and the egg yolks. Mix thoroughly. Spread the filling mixture over the batter and then cover the filling mixture with the remaining batter. Bake for 50 minutes. Serve with warm fruit sauce, sour cream or yogurt. Serves 8 to 10.

Exquisite Pound Cake

- 3 T. milk
- 3 large eggs
- 1 1/2 t. vanilla extract
- 1 1/2 c. cake flour, sifted
- 3/4 c. sugar
- 3/4 t. baking powder
- 1/4 t. salt
- 3/4 c. + 1 T. unsalted butter, softened

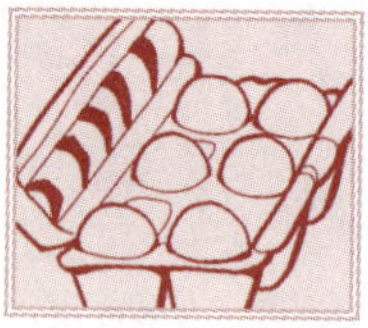

Preheat the convection oven to 325°F. Grease and flour an 8" x 4" loaf pan. In a medium bowl, combine the milk, eggs and the vanilla. In a large bowl, combine with an electric mixer on low speed, the cake flour, sugar, baking powder and the salt. Add the butter and half of the egg mixture to the flour mixture. Mix on low speed until the dry ingredients are moistened. Beat on medium speed for another minute. Scrape the sides of the bowl and gradually add the remaining egg mixture. Beat for another minute.

Pour the batter into the loaf pan, smoothing out the top surface. Bake for 50 minutes, or until a toothpick inserted in the middle of the cake comes out clean. After 30 minutes of baking, cover the loaf pan with a buttered piece of aluminum foil to prevent the cake from over browning.

Remove the cake from the oven and allow it to sit in the pan for 10 minutes. Invert it onto a greased wire rack to complete the cooling. Place the cake on a serving platter and sift powdered sugar over the top of the cake to finish. Serves 8.

Chocolate Kahlúa® Cake

- 18 1/2 oz. pkg. chocolate cake mix
- 1 c. Kahlúa®
- 1 c. sour cream
- 4 eggs
- 3/4 c. vegetable oil
- 1 12 oz. semi-sweet chocolate chips
- 1 c. walnuts, chopped

- 2/3 c. powdered sugar, sifted
- 2 T. Kahlúa®

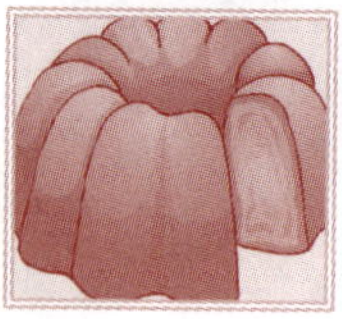

Preheat the convection oven to 325°F. Grease and flour a 12-cup bundt pan. Mix the chocolate cake mix, Kahlúa®, sour cream, eggs and the vegetable oil together thoroughly. Stir in the chocolate chips and the walnuts. Pour the batter into the bundt pan. Bake the cake for 55 to 60 minutes. Insert a wooden pick into the center of the cake. The pick will come out clean when the cake is finished. Remove the cake from the oven and let it sit for 10 minutes in the pan. Remove the cake to a wire rack to finish cooling. Place the cake on a serving platter.

Combine the sifted powdered sugar and the 2 tablespoons Kahlúa®. Drizzle this glaze slowly over the warm cake so that it is absorbed into the cake. Serves 10.

Pecan Rum Cake

Cake:

1 c. pecans or walnuts, chopped
18 1/2 oz. pkg. yellow cake mix
3 3/4 oz. instant vanilla pudding mix
4 eggs
1/2 c. cold water
1/2 c. vegetable oil
1/2 c. dark rum (80 proof)

Rum Glaze:

1/2 c. butter
1/4 c. water
1 c. sugar
1/2 c. dark rum (80 proof)

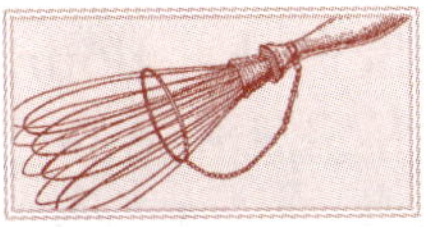

Preheat the convection oven to 325°F. Grease and flour a 12-cup bundt pan. Sprinkle the nuts over the bottom of the pan. Mix together the yellow cake mix, vanilla pudding mix, eggs, cold water, vegetable oil and the dark rum. Pour this batter over the nuts. Bake for 45 to 55 minutes. Cool for 10 minutes and then invert onto a serving plate.

In a small saucepan, melt the butter, water and the sugar. Boil for 5 minutes, stirring constantly. Remove from the heat and stir in the rum.

Poke the top of the cake with a fork. Drizzle the *Rum Glaze* slowly over the cake, allowing the glaze to be absorbed by the cake. Serves 10.

Fresh Strawberry Shortcake

2 c. all-purpose flour
1/4 c. sugar
4 t. baking powder
1/2 t. salt
pinch ground nutmeg
1/3 c. butter
1 egg, well beaten
1/3 c. milk
1 to 1 1/2 qt. fresh strawberries, cut into quarters
3/4 c. light brown sugar, packed
1 pt. whipping cream
butter as needed

Preheat the convection oven to 350°F. Generously butter a 9-inch round baking pan. Mix together the flour, sugar, baking powder, salt and nutmeg. Sift this mixture twice. Work in the butter with your fingertips. Add the egg and the milk. Combine just until the dry ingredients are moistened. Spoon the batter into the baking pan and pat it level. Bake for 15 minutes. Remove from the heat and cool 10 minutes. Invert the cake onto a wire rack and cut into 2 layers. Butter each layer.

One hour before serving, combine the quartered strawberries with the brown sugar. Place one layer of the shortcake, butter side up, on a serving platter.

Pile the strawberries on top of this layer. Next, place the remaining layer of shortcake, butter side down, on top of the strawberries. Drizzle with any remaining strawberry juice and top with whipped cream. Serves 8.

Green Apple & Walnut Cookies

1 apple, (Granny Smith or Pippin), peeled and cored
1 c. butter or margarine, melted
1 t. baking soda
1 1/2 c. brown sugar
2 T. honey or maple syrup
2 eggs
2 T. vanilla extract
3 t. ground cinnamon
1/2 c. walnuts, chopped
2 1/2 c. all-purpose flour

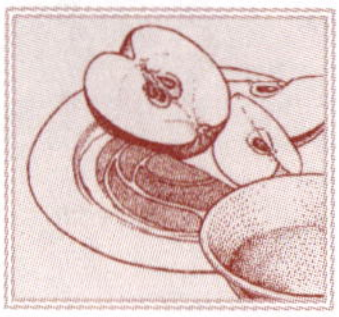

Preheat the convection oven to 300°F. Dice the apple into ⅜-inch cubes. Lay them on a baking sheet and bake for 15 minutes, until they are slightly soft. Let them cool.

Preheat the convection oven to 350°F. In a large bowl, combine the butter, baking soda, brown sugar, honey, eggs, vanilla and the cinnamon. Mix thoroughly. Add the apples and the walnuts and mix. Add the flour and mix completely. Add additional flour, if needed, until the cookie dough is not too sticky.

Place teaspoonfuls of dough onto the baking sheet and bake for 9 to 10 minutes. Do not overcook. These cookies should come out of the oven slightly undercooked for a delicious chewy texture. Makes 3 dozen.

Chocolate Almond Macaroons

1 c. semi-sweet chocolate chips
2 egg whites
8 oz. almond paste
1/3 c. powdered sugar, sifted
2 T. all-purpose flour

Chocolate Almond Topping:
1 c. semi-sweet chocolate chips
1 T. vegetable shortening
1/4 c. almonds, chopped

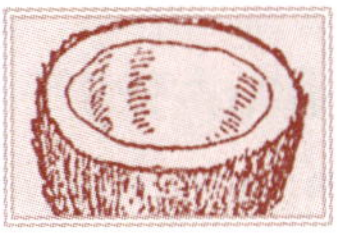

Preheat the convection oven to 300°F. Line 2 baking sheets with aluminum foil. Melt the chocolate chips over hot water or in the microwave oven on HIGH for 2 minutes. Stir until the chocolate is smooth. In a large bowl, combine the egg whites, almond paste, powdered sugar and the flour. Beat until this mixture is smooth. Blend in the melted chocolate. Spoon this batter into a pastry bag fitted with a rosette tip. Pipe 1¾-inch rosettes onto the baking sheets and bake for 25 minutes. Cool completely on wire racks.

Combine in a small bowl, ¾ cup of the chocolate chips and the shortening. Microwave on HIGH for 1 minute. Stir until the mixture is smooth. Drizzle each macaroon with ½ teaspoon of the chocolate. Sprinkle each cookie with chocolate chips and almonds. Makes 4 dozen.

One Big Chocolate Chip Cookie

- 1 1/4 c. all-purpose flour
- 1/4 t. baking soda
- 1/8 t. baking powder
- 1/4 t. salt
- 14 oz. semi-sweet chocolate chips, finely chopped
- 1 c. sugar
- 1/2 c. + 1 T. unsalted butter, cut into pieces
- 1/4 c. light corn syrup
- 1/4 c. water
- 3 eggs
- 1 T. vanilla extract
- 1 1/2 c. walnuts, chopped

Preheat the convection oven to 325°F. Line a 9" x 13" baking pan with a double layer of aluminum foil. Butter the bottom of the foil. In a large bowl, stir together the flour, baking soda, baking powder and salt. Set aside. Put the chocolate chips in a large heat-proof bowl.

In a medium saucepan, combine the sugar, butter, corn syrup and water. Cook until the butter melts, the sugar is dissolved and the mixture comes to a boil. Pour this hot syrup over the chocolate chips and let it melt the chips. Whisk together until it is smooth.

Add the eggs to the chocolate mixture, one at a time, whisking after each egg. Add in the vanilla and the flour mixture, whisking again until well-blended and smooth. Fold in the walnuts. Spread this batter into the prepared baking pan and bake for 40 to 50 minutes. Remove from the oven and cool. Cover the cookie with plastic wrap and let it sit for 6 hours before cutting. Makes 2 dozen individual cookies.

Favorite Chocolate Chip Oatmeal Cookies

1 c. vegetable shortening
3/4 c. sugar
3/4 c. light brown sugar
2 eggs, beaten
1 t. vanilla extract
1 3/4 c. all-purpose flour, sifted
1/2 t. salt
1 t. baking soda
2/3 c. quick cooking oats
1 c. walnuts, chopped
6 oz. semi-sweet chocolate chips

Preheat the convection oven to 350°F. In a mixing bowl, blend together the shortening, sugar and the light brown sugar. Add the eggs and the vanilla. Combine the flour, salt and the baking soda. Add this flour mixture to the egg mixture, combining thoroughly. Stir in the oats, walnuts and chocolate chips. Drop this batter by teaspoonfuls onto a baking sheet. Bake for 10 to 12 minutes. Remove from the oven and place on a wire rack to cool. Makes 4 dozen.

Coconut Macaroons

3 7-oz. pkgs. flaked coconut	2 t. vanilla extract
1 can sweetened condensed milk	1 1/2 t. almond extract

Preheat the convection oven to 325°F. Coat 2 cookie sheets with cooking spray. In a large bowl, combine the coconut, condensed milk, vanilla and almond extract. Mix well. Drop the dough by rounded spoonfuls onto the cookie sheets. Bake in the convection oven for 10 to 12 minutes, or until the cookies are browned around the edges. Remove from the oven and cool slightly. Place on wire racks to cool completely. Store loosely covered at room temperature. Makes 4 dozen.

Cookie Variations:

Chocolate Macaroons: Omit the almond extract and add 4 squares of melted unsweetened chocolate.

Chocolate Chip: Omit the almond extract and add 1 cup of the mini chocolate chips.

Mocha Cookies

- 4 oz. unsweetened chocolate, chopped
- 3 c. semi-sweet chocolate chips
- 1/2 c. unsalted butter, cut into pieces
- 1/2 c. all-purpose flour
- 1/2 t. baking powder
- 1/2 t. salt
- 4 large eggs, at room temperature
- 1 1/2 c. sugar
- 1 1/2 t. instant espresso or coffee powder
- 2 t. vanilla extract

Preheat the convection oven to 325°F. Line 2 baking sheets with parchment paper. In a metal bowl set over a saucepan of simmering water, melt the unsweetened chocolate, 1½ cups of the chocolate chips and the butter. Stir constantly until the mixture is smooth, then remove it from the heat.

In a small bowl, stir together the flour, baking powder and the salt. In a large bowl, cream the eggs and the sugar until the mixture is thick and pale. Beat in the espresso powder and the vanilla. Fold in the melted chocolate mixture. Add the flour mixture with the remaining chocolate chips. Stir well.

Let the batter sit for 15 minutes. Drop by heaping teaspoonfuls onto the baking sheets. Bake the cookies for 8 to 10 minutes. The cookies should puff up and their tops should be shiny and cracked. Let the cookies cool for 5 minutes on the baking sheets and then transfer them to wire racks to cool completely. Makes 3 dozen.

Mom's Lunchbox Cookies

6 T. butter
1/3 c. dark brown sugar
1/2 c. sugar
1 t. vanilla extract
1 egg
1 1/2 c. all-purpose flour
1/2 t. baking powder
1/2 t. baking soda
1/2 t. salt
1/2 t. ground ginger
1/2 t. ground cinnamon
2 c. rolled oats
2 1/2 t. orange marmalade
2/3 c. raisins

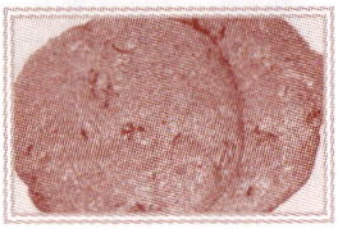

Preheat the convection oven to 325°F. Coat 2 cookie sheets with cooking spray.

Cream the butter with the sugars until light and fluffy. Beat in the vanilla and the egg. Sift the flour, baking powder, baking soda, salt and the spices together. Fold the flour mixture into the creamed butter mixture. Add the oats, marmalade and the raisins. Bake for 15 minutes. Remove from the oven and place on wire racks to cool. Makes 3 dozen.

Old-Fashioned Peanut Butter Cookies

1/2 c. butter or margarine
1/2 c. peanut butter
1/2 c. sugar
1/2 c. packed brown sugar
1 egg
1/2 t. vanilla extract
1 1/4 c. all-purpose flour, sifted
1/2 t. baking powder
3/4 t. baking soda
1/4 t. salt
granulated sugar

Lightly coat 2 cookie sheets with cooking spray. Thoroughly mix together the butter, peanut butter, sugars, egg and the vanilla. Sift the flour, baking powder, baking soda and the salt together. Add this flour mixture to the creamed mixture and combine well.

Chill the dough for 1 hour. Preheat the convection oven to 350°F. Roll the dough into balls the size of walnuts and place 3 inches apart on the cookie sheets. Flatten the balls with a fork to make a crisscross pattern. Bake for 10 to 12 minutes, or until the cookies are lightly browned. Sprinkle the tops of the cookies with a dusting of sugar and remove to a wire rack to cool. Makes 3 dozen.

Heartwarming Blackberry Cobbler

Filling:

5 c. fresh blackberries, rinsed and drained

3/4 c. sugar

3 T. cornstarch

1/4 t. salt

2 T. butter

Pastry:

1 c. all-purpose flour

1/2 t. salt

1/3 c. vegetable shortening

2 T. water

1 T. milk

1 T. sugar

Preheat the convection oven to 375°F. Pour the berries into the bottom of a 9-inch square baking pan. Combine the sugar, cornstarch and salt. Sprinkle the sugar mixture over the berries. Dot the top of the berries with butter. Set aside.

Combine the flour and salt in a medium bowl. Cut in the shortening until the mixture resembles coarse crumbs. Sprinkle with water and stir with a fork until the mixture holds together. Roll out the dough on a lightly floured surface.

Place the dough over the dish of berries, sealing the edges of the dough to the sides of the baking pan.

Cut slits in the top of the dough. Combine the milk and sugar, and brush over the top of the dough. Bake for 30 minutes, or until the crust is golden brown. Serve warm with your choice of ice cream. Serves 6.

Chocolate-Hazelnut Biscotti

- 4 oz. semi-sweet chocolate, coarsely chopped
- 1 c. packed light brown sugar
- 1 3/4 c. all-purpose flour
- 1/3 c. unsweetened cocoa
- 1 1/2 T. instant espresso powder
- 1 t. baking soda
- 1/4 t. salt
- 3 eggs
- 1 1/4 t. vanilla extract
- 1/2 t. almond extract
- 1 c. hazelnuts, toasted and coarsely chopped

Preheat the convection oven to 300°F. Line a baking sheet with parchment paper. In a food processor fitted with the metal blade, combine the chocolate and the brown sugar. Process until the chocolate is very fine. Set aside.

Sift together the flour, cocoa, espresso powder, baking soda and salt into a bowl. Set aside. Combine the eggs, vanilla and the almond extract in a large bowl. Using an electric mixer, beat the batter at medium speed to blend well. On low speed, add in the sugar and the flour mixtures. Beat slowly for 2 minutes and add the hazelnuts. Beat again until a stiff dough forms.

On a floured surface, divide the dough in half. Form each half into a log that is 12-inches long.

Transfer these logs to the baking sheet and pat into even, rounded shapes. Bake until almost firm to the touch, about 30 to 35 minutes. Remove from the oven and let the biscotti cool for 10 minutes.

Transfer the biscotti to a cutting board and cut the logs diagonally into 1-inch slices. Arrange the slices cut side down on the baking sheet. Bake an additional 20 minutes. Turn off the oven and allow the biscotti to cool completely in the oven with the oven door ajar. Serve or store in an airtight container. Makes 30 biscotti.

Gourmet Raspberry Brownies

3 oz. unsweetened chocolate
1/2 c. shortening
3 eggs
1 1/2 c. sugar
1 1/2 t. vanilla extract
1/4 t. salt
1 c. all-purpose flour
1 1/2 c. walnuts, chopped
1/3 c. raspberry preserves

Velvet Chocolate Glaze:
1 oz. unsweetened chocolate
2 T. butter
2 T. light corn syrup
2 T. powdered sugar
1 T. milk
2 t. vanilla extract

Preheat the convection oven to 300°F. Grease or spray with cooking spray an 8-inch square baking pan. Melt the chocolate with the shortening over warm water. Cool slightly. Blend together the eggs, sugar, vanilla and salt. Stir in the chocolate mixture. Add the flour and mix well. Fold in the walnuts. Pour the batter into the baking pan and bake for 40 minutes. Carefully spoon the preserves over the hot brownies. Cool and top with the *Velvet Chocolate Glaze*.

Melt the chocolate in the microwave oven on HIGH for 1 minute. Blend in the butter and the light corn syrup. Mix well and heat again for 30 seconds, if needed. Stir in the powdered sugar, milk and the vanilla. Mix until very smooth and glossy. Spread the glaze evenly over the brownies. Makes 12 brownies.

Delectable Shortbread Cookies

1 c. unsalted butter, at room temperature
3/4 c. powdered sugar, sifted
1 t. vanilla extract
2 c. all-purpose flour, sifted
1/2 t. salt

In a mixing bowl, cream the butter. Add the sugar and the vanilla and beat until the batter is smooth. In a smaller bowl, stir together the flour and the salt. Gently stir the flour into the butter mixture. Chill the dough for at least an hour.

Preheat the convection oven to 300°F. Line two baking sheets with parchment paper. On a lightly floured surface, roll out the dough to a ½-inch thickness. Cut the dough into rounds or use cookie cutters. Bake for 20 minutes, or until the cookies are dry, but not brown. Remove from the oven and cool on wire racks. Makes 2 dozen.

Delightful Lemon Bars

Crust:
2 c. all-purpose flour
1/3 c. powdered sugar
1 c. butter

Lemon Topping:
4 eggs
1/2 c. lemon juice
2 c. sugar
1/2 t. baking powder
1/4 c. flour
powdered sugar

Preheat the convection oven to 325°F. Sift together the flour and the powdered sugar. Cut the butter into the flour mixture until the mixture clings together. Press this into a 9" x 13" baking pan and bake for 20 to 25 minutes, or until the crust is lightly browned.

While the crust is baking, beat the eggs together with the sugar and the lemon juice. In a separate bowl, sift together the baking powder and the flour. Stir this flour mixture into the egg mixture. Pour the lemon filling over the baked crust. Bake the *Lemon Bars* for 25 minutes. Cool completely, cut into 24 bars and sprinkle with powdered sugar. Makes 24 bars.

Fresh Peach & Almond Crumble

- 10 to 12 fresh peaches, peeled and cored
- sugar to taste
- 3/4 c. raisins
- 1 c. all-purpose flour
- 1/2 c. sugar
- 1 c. ground almonds
- 1/4 c. butter

Preheat the convection oven to 375°F. Quarter the fresh peaches and place them in a greased 9" x 13" baking pan. Sprinkle the peaches with sugar and then layer the raisins on top of the peaches. In a separate bowl, combine together the flour, sugar, ground almonds and the butter. Spread this mixture over the fruit. Bake for 35 minutes until the top is lightly browned. Serve warm. Serves 6 to 8.

Spiced Pear Pralines

1/2 c. packed brown sugar
1/3 c. all-purpose flour
1/4 c. butter or margarine, melted
3/4 c. pecans, chopped
1 9-inch unbaked pie shell
1 large can pear halves
1/2 t. lemon rind, grated
1/2 t. ground ginger
1/2 t. ground cinnamon

Preheat the convection oven to 375°F. In a mixing bowl, combine the brown sugar, flour, butter and the pecans to make a crumb mixture. Spread ½ of this mixture onto the bottom of the pie crust. Arrange the pear halves on top of the crumb mixture. Sprinkle the lemon rind and the spices over the pear halves. Cover the top with the remaining crumb mixture. Bake for 30 to 40 minutes or until the crust is light brown. Serve warm. Serves 8.

Three-Fruit Cobbler

2 T. unsalted butter
1 lb. apples, peeled, cored and sliced
1 lb. peaches, fresh or frozen, peeled and sliced
1 c. blueberries, fresh or frozen
2 T. fresh lemon juice
1/2 c. sugar
11/2 t. all-purpose flour
1 t. vanilla extract
2 c. all-purpose flour
1/4 c. sugar
2 t. baking powder
1/4 t. salt
2 T. butter, cut into small cubes
1/2 t. ground ginger
1 T. orange zest
1 c. heavy cream

In a large frying pan over medium heat, melt the butter. Stir in the apples, peaches, blueberries, lemon juice, sugar and the flour. Cover partially and cook until tender, about 15 to 20 minutes. Stir in the vanilla. Transfer this fruit mixture to a buttered 10-inch deep dish pie pan.

Preheat the convection oven to 400°F. Combine the 2 cups flour, sugar, baking powder and the salt. Cut in the butter until the mixture resembles coarse crumbs. Stir in the ginger. Stir the orange zest into the cream. Stir the cream mixture into the crumb mixture with a fork just until the dough holds together. On a lightly floured surface, knead the dough once and then roll out to ½-inch larger than the size of the deep dish pie pan. Transfer the dough to the dish and trim off any excess dough. Cut a hole in the center of the dough. Brush the dough with additional cream. Bake for 10 minutes, then reduce the oven to 375°F and bake for an additional 20 to 25 minutes. Serve warm. Serves 6 to 8.

Sugar Crumb Crispy Crescents

Rolls:
3 T. butter or margarine, softened
1/4 c. sugar
1/4 c. packed brown sugar
1 t. ground cinnamon
1/8 t. salt
1/2 c. all-purpose flour
8 oz. tube crescent dinner rolls

Glaze:
1/2 c. powdered sugar
1/2 t. vanilla extract
1 T. milk

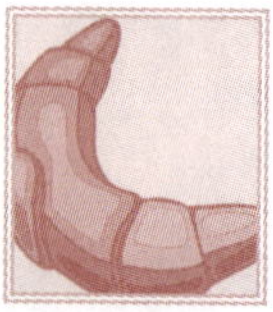

Preheat the convection oven to 375°F. Lightly coat a baking sheet with cooking spray. In a small bowl, combine the butter, sugars, cinnamon, salt and the flour. Mix until the flour and butter are crumbly. Separate the crescent roll dough into 8 triangles. Sprinkle each triangle with the crumb mixture and place on the baking sheet. Bake for 10 minutes until lightly browned.

Combine the powdered sugar, vanilla and the milk until smooth. Brush the glaze over the warm triangles. Serve these crispy crescents warm. Serves 8.

Cappuccino Tarts

2 eggs
2 T. coffee liqueur
1 T. sugar
1 c. milk
2 t. instant coffee granules
1/8 t. ground cinnamon
12 3-inch tart shells

Preheat the convection oven to 325°F. In a small bowl, beat together the eggs, coffee liqueur and the sugar. In a small saucepan, combine the milk and the coffee granules. Heat over medium-high heat for 2 to 3 minutes until the milk is steaming and tiny bubbles appear around the edge of the saucepan. Beat the milk mixture into the egg mixture.

Strain the egg mixture through a sieve into a pitcher. Carefully pour the egg mixture into the tart shells, filling evenly. The tart shells will be very full. Sprinkle each tart with a little of the cinnamon. Bake for 20 to 25 minutes until the filling is set and the tart shells are golden brown. Cool before serving. Makes 12 tarts.

Raisin Bread Pudding with Hard Sauce

1 loaf of stale French bread
1 qt. milk
2 T. butter, softened
3 eggs
1 1/2 c. sugar
2 T. vanilla extract
1 c. raisins

Hard Sauce:
1/2 c. butter, softened
1 c. powdered sugar
1 egg
zest and juice of one lemon

Preheat the convection oven to 325°F. Grease a 9" x 13" baking pan with 2 tablespoons of butter. Crumble the bread into a large bowl and pour the milk over it. Allow this to rest for 5 minutes.

In a medium bowl, beat together the eggs, sugar and the vanilla. Stir this mixture into the bread and then add the raisins. Pour the batter into the prepared baking dish. Bake until browned and set, about 45 to 50 minutes. If the pudding browns too quickly, place a piece of aluminum foil over the top. Remove the pudding from the heat and serve warm with the sauce.

In the top of a double boiler, stir together the butter and the powdered sugar until the sugar is dissolved and the mixture is very hot. Remove it from the heat. Beat the egg well and whisk it into the sugar mixture. Continue whisking until the mixture has cooled to room temperature. Add the zest and the lemon juice to taste. Serve the sauce on the side. Serves 8 to 10.

Southern Sweet Potato Pie

4 sweet potatoes
2 eggs
1 c. sugar
1 t. vanilla extract
1/8 t. salt
1/2 t. ground nutmeg
1/2 c. butter, softened
1/2 c. evaporated milk
1 9-inch unbaked pie crust
1 pt. heavy cream, whipped

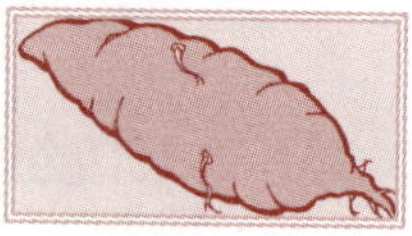

Preheat the oven to 325°F. Boil the sweet potatoes for 15 minutes, or until they are soft. Peel and beat until they are smooth. Add the eggs, sugar, vanilla, salt, nutmeg, butter and evaporated milk. Beat until the mixture is creamy. Pour this mixture into the pie shell. Bake for 20 minutes. If a knife inserted in the center comes out clean, the pie is done. Bake another 5-10 minutes, if needed. Serve warm with whipping cream. Serves 6 to 8.

Granola Apple Crisp

- 3 tart apples, peeled, cored and chopped
- 1 c. sugar
- 2 T. lemon juice
- 2 T. all-purpose flour
- 1/4 c. water
- 1 c. flour
- 1 c. brown sugar
- 1 c. prepared granola
- 1 c. butter, melted
- 1/2 c. walnuts, chopped
- 1 t. ground cinnamon
- 1/2 t. ground cloves

Preheat the convection oven to 325°F. Coat a 9-inch pie pan with cooking spray. In a large bowl, combine the apples, sugar, lemon juice, flour and water. Pour the apple mixture into the pie pan. Mix together the flour, brown sugar, granola, butter, walnuts, cinnamon and cloves. Pour the flour mixture over the apples completely. Bake for 35 minutes, or until the apples are tender. Serve warm. Serves 8.

Dream Bar Pecan Pie

1 9-inch unbaked pie shell
3 eggs
2 T. butter or margarine, melted
1 c. packed brown sugar
2/3 c. quick cooking oats
2/3 c. shredded coconut
1/2 c. milk
1 t. vanilla extract
1/2 c. pecans, chopped
8 to 10 unbroken pecans

Preheat the convection oven to 375°F. Make holes in the pie shell with a fork. Bake the pie shell for 5 to 6 minutes until the crust is barely browned. Remove the crust to a wire rack and cool slightly.

Reduce the convection oven to 300°F. Beat together in a large bowl, the eggs and the butter. Add the brown sugar, oatmeal, shredded coconut, milk, vanilla and the chopped pecans. Pour the filling into the pie crust. Place the pecans around the edge of the filling to decorate. Bake for 35 minutes, or until the pie filling is set. Serve warm or cool. Serves 8 to 10.

Homestyle Buttermilk Cake

2 c. sugar

3/4 c. butter or margarine, softened

3 c. all-purpose flour

1 t. baking soda

2 T. cocoa

1/2 t. ground cloves

1/2 t. ground allspice

1 t. ground cinnamon

2 c. buttermilk

1/2 c. pecans, chopped

powdered sugar

Preheat the convection oven to 325°F. Grease a 12-cup bundt pan. In a large mixing bowl, combine the sugar and the butter. In a separate bowl, mix together the flour, baking soda, cocoa, cloves, allspice and cinnamon. Add this flour mixture alternately with the buttermilk to the sugar/butter mixture and blend well. Stir in the pecans. Pour the batter into the bundt pan. Bake for 30 to 35 minutes. Remove the cake from the oven, cool for 10 minutes in the pan, and then invert onto a serving plate. Sprinkle with sifted powdered sugar. Serves 10.

CHAPTER EIGHT

The Convection Oven Roasting Guide & Basic Food Cooking Chart

THE CONVECTION OVEN ROASTING GUIDE

Bake at 325°F.

Food	Baking Time per Pound of Meat	Internal Temp. Of the Meat
BEEF:		
Roast 3 to 4 lbs.	20 to 25 minutes	140° rare 160° medium 170° well
5 to 6 lbs.	30 to 35 minutes	140° rare 160° medium 170° well
Tenderloin 3 to 4 lbs.	15 to 20 minutes	140° rare
PORK:		
Tenderloin 1 to 2 lbs.	15 to 20 minutes	170°
Boneless Top 2 to 4 lbs.	25 to 30 minutes	170°
Crown 4 to 6 lbs.	30 to 35 minutes	170°
Ham, fully cooked 5 to 7 lbs.	15 to 18 minutes	140°

Bake at 325°F.

Food	Baking Time per Pound of Meat	Internal Temp. Of the Meat
LAMB:		
Shoulder 3 to 5 lbs.	35 to 40 minutes	175° to 180°
Crown Roast 4 to 6 lbs.	35 to 40 minutes	175° to 180°
Leg 5 to 8 lbs.	25 to 30 minutes	175° to 180°
VEAL:		
Loin 4 to 6 lbs.	25 to 30 minutes	170°
Rolled Rump 3 to 5 lbs.	35 to 40 minutes	170°
Rolled Shoulder 4 to 6 lbs.	35 to 40 minutes	170°
TURKEY:		
Whole 14 to 16 lbs.	15 to 18 minutes	185°
Boneless 3 to 5 lbs.	25 to 30 minutes	170°
CHICKEN:		
Whole Fryer 3 to 4 lbs.	25 to 30 minutes	175°

THE BASIC FOOD COOKING CHART

Food Type	Oven Temperature: Degrees Farenheit	Time
Breakfast casseroles and eggs	325°	35 to 45 minutes
Breakfast breads and muffins	325° to 350°	20 to 25 minutes
Roasts	325°	See Roasting Guide
One-Dish meals	325° to 350°	25 to 30 minutes
Pizzas	375° to 400°	15 minutes
Fish dishes	350° to 375°	15 to 20 minutes
Roasted vegetables	400°	12 to 15 minutes
Baked Potatoes	375°	40 to 45 minutes
Frittatas	325°	20 to 25 minutes
Baked vegetable dishes	350° to 375°	20 to 25 minutes
Muffins	350° to 375°	15 to 20 minutes

THE BASIC FOOD COOKING CHART

Food Type	Oven Temperature: Degrees Farenheit	Time
Quick Breads	325° to 350°	30 to 45 minutes
Soufflés	325°	40 to 50 minutes
Cakes	350°	30 to 35 minutes
Cookies	325° to 350°	10 to 15 minutes
Macaroons and shortbread cookies	300° to 325°	8 to 10 minutes
Cobblers and crumbles	375°	25 to 35 minutes
Pies and puddings	325°	30 to 35 minutes

PERSONAL RECIPE NOTES

PERSONAL RECIPE NOTES

PERSONAL RECIPE NOTES

PERSONAL RECIPE NOTES

PERSONAL RECIPE NOTES